Eyewitness
CRYSTAL & GEM

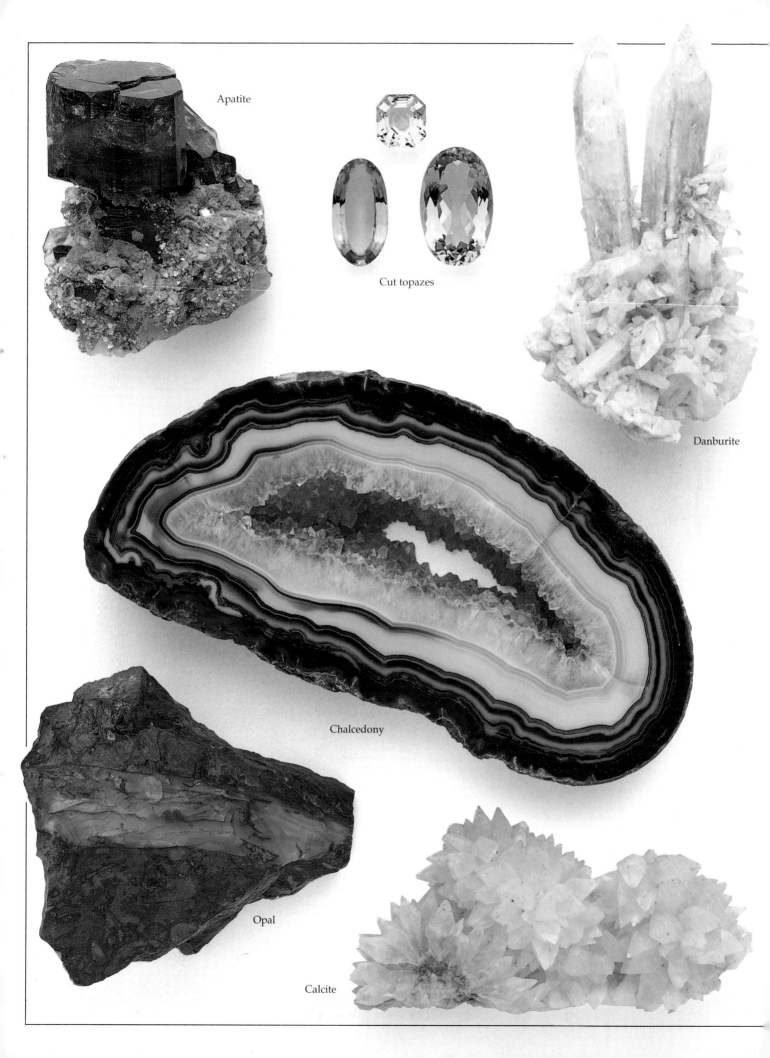

Apatite

Cut topazes

Danburite

Chalcedony

Opal

Calcite

Sphaerocobaltite

Eyewitness
CRYSTAL
& GEM

Crocoite

In association with
THE NATURAL HISTORY MUSEUM

Written by
Dr R. F. SYMES and Dr R.R. HARDING

Dumortierite
bottle

Cut garnets

Cut tourmalines

Aragonite

Microcline

Meta-tobernite

Dorling Kindersley

Malachite

Gold

Cut tourmaline

Cut topaz

Cut sapphire

Crocoite

Agate

Mother of pearl

Tourmaline

Agate

DK

LONDON, NEW YORK, MUNICH,
MELBOURNE, and DELHI

Project editor Louise Pritchard
Art editor Thomas Keenes
Senior editor Helen Parker
Senior art editors Julia Harris, Jacquie Gulliver
Production Louise Barrat
Picture research Cynthia Hole
Special photography Colin Keates ABIPP
(Natural History Museum)

PAPERBACK EDITION
Managing editor Andrew Macintyre
Managing art editor Jane Thomas
Editor and reference compiler Angela Wilkes
Art editor Catherine Goldsmith
Production Jenny Jacoby
Picture research Marie Osborn
DTP designer Siu Yin Ho
2 4 6 8 10 9 7 5 3

This Eyewitness ® Guide has been conceived by
Dorling Kindersley Limited and Editions Gallimard

Hardback edition first published in Great Britain in 1991.
This edition published in Great Britain in 2002
by Dorling Kindersley Limited,
80 Strand, London WC2R ORL

A CIP catalogue record for this book is
available from the British Library.

ISBN 0 7513 4743 4

Colour reproduction by
Colourscan, Singapore
Printed in Hong Kong by Toppan

See our complete
catalogue at

www.dk.com

Contents

Amethyst

MA	MB	MC
3	05		
MD	ME	MF
MG	MH	MM
MN	MO	MR
AB	MT	MW

What is a crystal?

Crystals are associated with perfection, transparency, and clarity. Many crystals fit these ideals, especially those cut as gemstones, but most are neither perfect nor transparent. Crystals are solid materials in which the atoms are arranged in a regular pattern (pp. 14–15). Many substances can grow in characteristic geometric forms enclosed by smooth plane surfaces. They are said to have crystallized, and the plane surfaces are known as faces. The word crystal is based on the Greek word *krystallos*, derived from *kryos* meaning icy cold. In ancient times it was thought that rock crystal, a colourless variety of quartz, was ice that had frozen so hard it would never melt.

STATES OF MATTER
A material can exist as a solid, a liquid, or a gas depending on its temperature. Water is made of atoms of hydrogen and oxygen bound together to form molecules. In the vapour (steam) the molecules move about vigorously; in the liquid they move slowly; in the solid (ice) they are arranged in a regular order and form a crystalline solid. These ice crystals are about 450 times their real size.

FAMILIAR FACES
These magnificent crystals have formed from hot watery solutions within the Earth. They show characteristic faces.

Tourmaline
crystal

Quartz crystal

Albite
crystals

CRYSTAL MINORITY
Most crystals in this book are of naturally occurring, solid, inorganic materials called minerals. But inorganic compounds not found naturally as minerals also form crystals, such as this artificially grown crystal of potassium magnesium sulphate.

MASSIVE MINERAL
Crystals only grow large and perfect in the right conditions. Most grow irregularly and the faces are often difficult to distinguish. This specimen of the mineral scapolite consists of a mass of small, poorly formed crystals. Minerals in this form are described as massive.

GLASS HOUSE
The Crystal Palace was built for the Great Exhibition of London of 1851, but was destroyed by fire in 1936. The roof and outer walls were made of nearly 300,000 panes of glass – not crystals.

Pyrolusite dendrites

CRYSTAL LINING
These fern-like growths look like a plant but are in fact crystalline growths of the mineral pyrolusite. Such crystals are called dendrites (p. 21) and are often found lining joints and cracks in rocks.

18th-century miniature painting of an Indian woman bedecked with jewellery

Cut heliodor (pp. 38–39)

GEM OF A CRYSTAL
Most gemstones are natural crystals chosen for their beauty, durability, and in many instances rarity. They are usually cut and polished (pp. 58–59). Crystals with the same composition and properties as naturally occurring minerals can now be grown artificially (pp. 26–27) and cut as gemstones.

Cut aquamarine (pp. 38–39)

POTATO SURPRISE
Crystals often occur in places where you would least expect to find them. In certain ploughed fields of southern England, irregular nodules known as "potato stones" are found. When broken open they often reveal sparkling crystals.

MOST IRREGULAR
Some of the objects which we know as "crystal" are glass and are not truly crystalline. Glass has little structure, as it is cooled too quickly for the atoms to arrange themselves into a regular order, and is said to be amorphous.

A world of crystals

CRYSTALS ARE ALL AROUND US. We live on a crystal planet in a crystal world. The rocks which form the Earth, the moon, and meteorites, pieces of rock from space, are made up of minerals and virtually all of these minerals are made up of crystals. Minerals are naturally occurring crystalline solids composed of atoms of various elements. The most important of these are oxygen, silicon, and six common metallic elements including iron and calcium. Crystalline particles make up mountains and form the ocean floors. When we cross the beach we tread on crystals. We use them at home (pp. 62–63) and at work (pp. 28–29), indeed crystals are vital to today's technology.

CRYSTAL LAYERS
The Earth is formed of three layers: the crust, the mantle, and the core. These are made mostly of solid rock-forming minerals. Some rocks, such as pure marble and quartzite, are made of just one mineral, but most are made of two or more.

Orthoclase

Quartz

Biotite

GRANITE
The most characteristic rock of the Earth's outermost layer, the continental crust, is granite. It consists mainly of the minerals quartz, feldspar, and mica. This specimen shows very large crystals of the feldspar mineral orthoclase, with small crystals of quartz and biotite mica.

ECLOGITE
The Earth's upper mantle is probably mostly peridotite but other rocks include dunite and eclogite. This specimen, originally from the mantle, is eclogite containing green pyroxene and small garnets.

Garnet crystal

METEORITE
It is thought that the centre of the Earth, the inner core, may be similar in composition to this iron meteorite. It has been cut, polished, and acid-etched to reveal its crystalline structure.

LIQUID ROCK
Molten lava from inside the Earth can erupt from volcanoes such as the Kilauea volcano, Hawaii, shown here. When the lava cools, minerals crystallize and it becomes a solid rock.

CRYSTAL STRENGTH
Most buildings are made of crystals. Natural rock and artificial materials are both mostly crystalline, and the strength of cement depends on the growth of crystals.

DOWN TO DUST
Pebbles, sand, and the greater part of soil are all formed from eroded rocks. Eventually, they will be eroded even further to form dust in the air (p. 32). Like the rocks they come from, these familiar things are all made up of crystals.

Quartzite pebbles

Feldspar crystal

Basalt pebble

Quartz sand grains

Soil

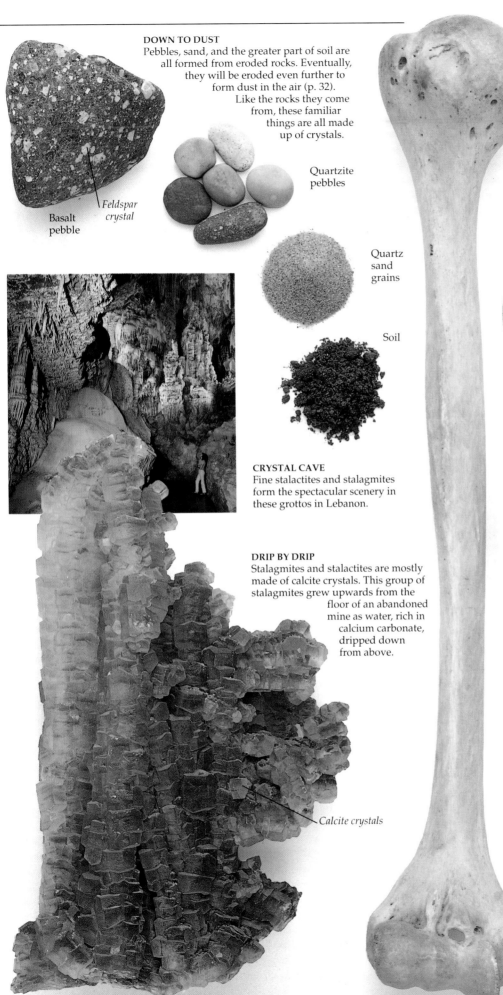

CRYSTAL CAVE
Fine stalactites and stalagmites form the spectacular scenery in these grottos in Lebanon.

DRIP BY DRIP
Stalagmites and stalactites are mostly made of calcite crystals. This group of stalagmites grew upwards from the floor of an abandoned mine as water, rich in calcium carbonate, dripped down from above.

Calcite crystals

Organic crystals
Crystals do not only grow in rocks. The elements that make up most rock-forming minerals are also important to life on Earth. For example, minerals such as calcite and apatite crystallize inside plants and animals.

MICROCRYSTALS
This microscope picture of a diatom, *Cyclotella pseudostelligera*, shows a symmetrical structure. Diatoms are microscopic algae whose cell walls are made up of tiny silica crystals.

ANIMAL MINERAL
Gallstones sometimes form inside an animal's gall bladder. This gallstone from a cow has exactly the same crystalline composition as struvite, a naturally occurring mineral.

STRESSFUL
Adrenalin is a hormone, a substance produced by the body to help it cope with stress. This greatly enlarged picture of adrenalin shows it is crystalline.

HUMAN APATITE
Bones contain tiny crystals of the mineral apatite. They make up the skeleton in vertebrate mammals – those that have a backbone, such as humans and horses. This is a human humerus (upper arm bone).

Natural beauty

W<small>ELL-FORMED CRYSTALS</small> are objects of great beauty and extreme rarity. Conditions have to be just right for them to grow (pp. 20–21) and any later changes in conditions must act to protect rather than destroy them. Even if they do grow and survive, many are destroyed by people during mining and other activities. Survivors are therefore of great interest. The crystals shown are about 60 per cent their real size.

PROUSTITE
Crystals of cherry-red proustite are known as ruby silvers and are often found associated with silver deposits. This exceptional group was collected from a famous silver mine area at Chanarcillo, Copiapo, Chile. The mines were extensively worked between 1830 and 1880.

BOURNONITE
These magnificent bright-grey "cog-wheel" crystals were collected from the Herodsfoot lead mine, near Liskeard in Cornwall, England. Between 1850 and 1875 this mine produced bournonite crystals of a quality still unsurpassed elsewhere.

Crystal Dream, a science fiction creation which the French artist Jean Giraud, known as Moebius, based on crystal shapes

TOPAZ
This perfect topaz crystal was one of many wonderful crystals that were found in the last century close to the Urulga River in the remote areas of the Borshchovochny Mountains in Siberia. Most were sherry coloured and some weighed up to 10 kg (22 lb).

Giant rock crystal and smoky quartz crystal, as found inside cavities in certain rocks, especially in Brazil

EPIDOTE
This is one of the finest epidote crystals known, as it shows good colour and fine prismatic habit (p. 23) for a crystal of this species. It was collected from a small working high in the mountains in Austria. This mineral site was said to have been discovered by a mountain guide in 1865.

BARYTE
The iron-mining areas of Cumbria, England are renowned for the quality of their baryte crystals. The crystals display a range of colours and each colour comes mostly from one mine. These golden-yellow crystals came from the Dalmellington mine, Frizington, where many fine specimens were collected during the 19th century.

BENITOITE
These triangular-shaped, sapphire-blue crystals of benitoite (p. 49) were found close to the San Benito River, California, USA. Such crystals have not been found in such quantity or quality anywhere else in the world.

Beautifully formed beryl crystals from various parts of the world

CALCITE
One of the most common and widely distributed minerals is calcite. It occurs as crystals in many different shapes and shades of colour. Some of the most beautiful calcite crystal groups came from the Egremont iron mining area of Cumbria, England in the late 19th century. This typical example consists of many fine colourless crystals, some of which are slightly tinged with red.

Crystals – outside…

A WELL FORMED CRYSTAL has certain regular (symmetrical) features. One feature is that sets of faces have parallel edges. Another feature of many crystals is that for every face, there is a parallel face on the opposite side. Crystals may have three types of symmetry. If a crystal can be divided into two, so that each half is a mirror image of the other, the line that divides them is called a "plane of symmetry". If a crystal is rotated about an imaginary straight line and the same pattern of faces appears a number of times in one turn, then the line is an "axis of symmetry". Depending on how many times the pattern appears, symmetry about an axis is described as twofold, threefold, fourfold, or sixfold. If a crystal is entirely bounded by pairs of parallel faces then it has a "centre of symmetry".

IN CONTACT
A contact goniometer is used to measure the angles between crystal faces. The Law of Constancy of Angle states that in all crystals of the same substance, the angles between corresponding faces are always the same.

Scale from which interfacial angle is read

Topaz crystal in position for measuring

Romé de l'Isle (1736-90), who established the Law of Constancy of Angle first proposed by the scientist Steno in 1669

Cubic system represented by galena. Essential symmetry element: four threefold axes.

SEVEN SYSTEMS
Crystals have differing amounts of symmetry and are placed, according to this, in one of seven major categories called systems. Crystals in the cubic system have the highest symmetry. The most symmetrical have 9 planes, 12 axes, and a centre of symmetry. Crystals in the triclinic system have the least symmetry with only a centre of symmetry or no symmetry at all.

Tetragonal system represented by idocrase. Essential symmetry element: one fourfold axis.

Orthorhombic system represented by baryte. Essential symmetry element: three twofold axes.

Crystal in posititon for measuring

ON REFLECTION
Made in about 1860, this optical goniometer is designed to measure the interfacial angles of small crystals by the reflection of light from their faces. The crystal is rotated until a reflection of light is seen from two adjacent faces. The angle between the two faces is read off the graduated circle on the right.

Monoclinic system represented by orthoclase (twinned). Essential symmetry element: one twofold axis.

Triclinic system represented by axinite. No axis of symmetry.

Hexagonal system represented by beryl. Essential symmetry: one sixfold axis.

SAME BUT DIFFERENT
Some crystallographers (studiers of crystals) consider that the trigonal system is part of the hexagonal system. They both have the same set of axes but the trigonal has only threefold symmetry. This is seen in the terminal faces.

Trigonal system represented by calcite. Essential symmetry: one threefold axis.

DESIGNED FOR SYMMETRY
This maple leaf design is one of 13 made to commemorate the 13th Congress of the International Union of Crystallography held in Canada in 1981. The repetitive designs were based on the elements of crystal symmetry.

Triclinic model

Cubic model

MODEL CRYSTALS
Crystal models were made to help crystallographers understand symmetry. These glass models were made in about 1900 in Germany. They contain cotton threads strung between the faces to show axes of rotation.

Hexagonal model

Form

Crystals of the same mineral may not look alike. The same faces on two crystals may be different sizes and therefore form different-shaped crystals. Crystals may also grow with a variation of "form". Shown here are three forms found in the cubic crystal system, illustrated by pyrite.

Studies of the transformation of geometrical bodies from Leonardo da Vinci's sketch book

CUBE
A form of six square faces that make 90° angles with each other. Each face intersects one of the four-fold axes and is parallel to the other two.

OCTAHEDRON
A form of eight equilateral triangular faces, each of which intersects all three of the four-fold axes equally.

PYRITOHEDRON
This form consists of 12 five-sided faces. It is also known as a pentagonal dodecahedron.

Dodecahedral face

Octahedral face

Cubic face

Below: Diagram to show the relationship between different cubic forms

Octahedron

Cube and octahedron

Cube

Cube and pyritohedron

Pyritohedron

COMBINATION OF FORMS
These crystals show cubic faces combined with octahedral faces with poorly developed dodecahedral faces blending into the cubic faces.

...and inside

THE INTERNAL ATOMIC STRUCTURE of crystals determines their regular shape and other properties. Each atom has its own special position and is tied to others by bonding forces. The atoms of a particular mineral always group in the same way to form crystals of that mineral. In early crystallography, the study of crystals, one of the most significant deductions was made by the Abbé Hauy (p. 15) in 1784. In 1808, Dalton defined his theory that matter was built up from tiny particles called atoms. In 1895, Röntgen discovered X-rays and, in 1912, von Laue (p. 15) realized that these might help determine the arrangement of atoms within a solid. This was the start of our understanding of the inside of crystals.

NOT CARBON COPIES
Diamond and graphite are both formed from the chemical element carbon, but there are striking differences between them in properties. This is explained by their different internal structures.

Diamond set in a ring

Graphite pencil

Graphite

Structural model of graphite

GRAPHITE
In graphite, carbon atoms are linked in a hexagonal arrangement in widely spaced layers. The layers are only weakly bonded and can slip easily over one another, making graphite one of the softest minerals.

Diamond crystal

DIAMOND
In diamond, each carbon atom is strongly bonded to four others to form a rigid compact structure. This structure makes diamond much harder than graphite.

Structural model of diamond

Augite crystal

ACTINOLITE
Silicate minerals, present in all common rocks apart from limestone, have a basic unit of a tetrahedron of one silicon and four oxygen atoms (SiO_4). Actinolite, a member of the amphibole group of minerals, has a structure based on a double chain of these tetrahedra.

GOLD ATOMS
Crystalline solids have a complex lattice-work of atoms. This photograph shows the atomic lattice of gold magnified millions of times. Each yellow blob represents an individual atom.

Model showing SiO_4 tetrahedra in a single-chain silicate

Oxygen atom

Silicon atom

AUGITE
An important group of silicate minerals is the pyroxenes, including augite. Their internal structure is based on a single chain of SiO_4 tetrahedra.

Model showing SiO_4 tetrahedra in a double-chain silicate

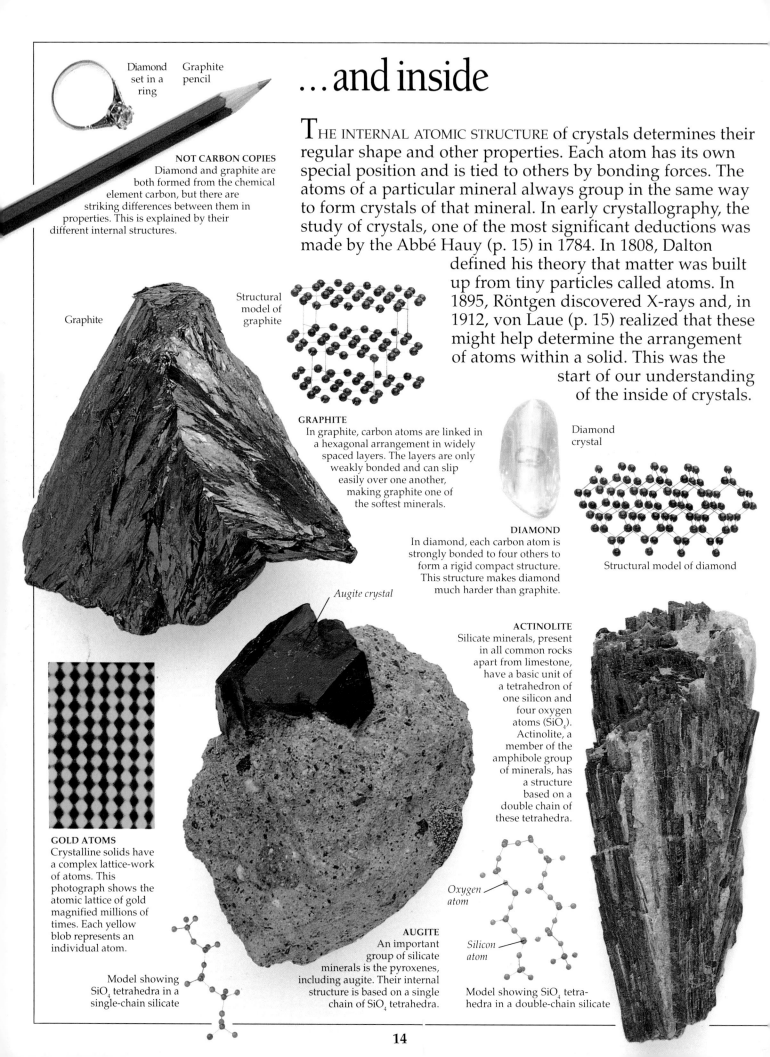

BERYL
In some silicate minerals, the internal structure is based on groups of three, four, or six SiO$_4$ tetrahedra linked in rings. Beryl (pp. 38–39) has rings made of groups of six tetrahedra.

MAX VON LAUE (1879–1960)
Laue showed with X-ray photographs that crystals were probably made of planes of atoms.

Wavelength (metres)	
10^{-15}	Gamma rays
10^{-11}	
10^{-9}	X-rays
10^{-7}	Ultraviolet radiation
10^{-6}	Visible light
10^{-4}	Infrared radiation (heat)
1	Microwaves
10^{5}	Radio waves

Decreasing wavelength

ELECTRO-MAGNETIC WAVES
X-rays are part of the electromagnetic radiation spectrum. All radiations can be described in terms of waves, many of which, such as light, radio, and heat, are familiar. The waves differ only in length and frequency. White light, which is visible to the human eye, is composed of electromagnetic waves varying in wavelength between red and violet in the spectrum (p. 16), but these visible rays are only a fraction of the whole spectrum.

X-RAY PHOTO
This Laue photograph shows the diffraction of a beam of X-rays by a beryl crystal. The symmetrical pattern is related to the hexagonal symmetry of the crystal.

Cleavage

Some crystals split along well-defined planes called cleavage planes which are characteristic for all specimens of that species. They form along the weakest plane in the structure and are direct evidence of the orderly arrangement of atoms.

TOPAZ
This fine blue topaz crystal from Madagascar shows a perfect cleavage. Topaz is one of a group of silicates with isolated SiO$_4$ groups in their structure.

Cleavage plane

MICA
The micas are a group of silicate minerals which have a sheet structure. The atomic bonding perpendicular to the sheet structure is weak and cleavage occurs easily along these planes.

Thin cleavage flakes

THE ABBÉ HAUY (1743–1822)
Hauy realized that crystals had a regular shape because of an inner regularity. He had seen how calcite often fractures into rhombs, along cleavage planes, and decided crystals were built up by regularly stacked building blocks similar to these.

QUARTZ
The structure of quartz is based on a strongly bonded, three-dimensional network of silicon and oxygen atoms. Crystals do not cleave easily but show a rounded, concentric fracture known as conchoidal.

The colour of crystals

MOONSTONES
The most familiar gem variety of the feldspar minerals is moonstone (p. 45). The white or blue sheen is caused by layers of tiny crystals of albite within orthoclase.

THE COLOUR OF A CRYSTAL can be its most striking feature. The causes of colour are varied and many minerals occur in a range of colours. Something looks a particular colour largely due to your eye and brain reacting to different wavelengths of light (p. 15). When white light (daylight) falls on a crystal some of the wavelengths may be reflected, and some absorbed. If some are absorbed, those remaining will make up a colour other than white because some of the wavelengths that make up white light are missing. Sometimes light is absorbed and re-emitted without changing and the mineral will appear colourless.

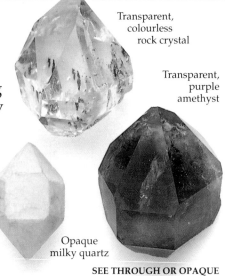

Transparent, colourless rock crystal

Transparent, purple amethyst

Opaque milky quartz

SEE THROUGH OR OPAQUE
Crystals can be transparent (they let through nearly all the light and can be seen right through), translucent (they let some light through but cannot be seen through clearly), or opaque (they do not let any light through and cannot be seen through at all). Most gemstones are transparent but can be coloured or colourless.

Idiochromatic

Some minerals are nearly always the same colour because certain light-absorbing atoms are an essential part of their crystal structure. These minerals are described as idio-chromatic. For example, copper minerals are nearly always red, green, or blue according to the nature of the copper present.

ISAAC NEWTON (1642–1727)
Sir Isaac Newton was an English scientist who achieved great fame for his work on, among other things, the nature of white light. He discovered that white light can be separated into seven different colours, and followed this with an explanation of the theory of the rainbow.

The colours known as the spectrum, produced by dispersion of white light in a prism

SULPHUR
Sulphur is an idiochromatic mineral and normally crystallizes in bright yellow crystals. These are often found as encrusting masses around volcanic vents and fumaroles (p. 20).

AZURITE
Azurite is a copper mineral which is always a shade of blue – hence the term azure blue. In ancient times it was crushed and used as a pigment.

Allochromatic

A large number of minerals occur in a wide range of colours caused by impurities or light-absorbing defects in the atomic structure. For example, quartz, diamond, beryl, and corundum can be red, green, yellow, and blue. These minerals are described as allochromatic.

RHODOCHROSITE
Manganese minerals such as rhodochrosite are normally pink or red. The bright red colour of some beryls is due to minute amounts of manganese.

ERYTHRITE
Cobalt minerals such as erythrite are usually pink or reddish. Trace amounts of cobalt may colour normally colourless minerals.

FLUORITE
Some minerals when exposed to invisible ultra-violet light (p. 15), emit visible light of various colours. This is called fluorescence, normally caused by foreign atoms called activators in the crystal structure. The fluorescent colour of a mineral is usually different from its colour in daylight. This fluorite crystal is green in daylight.

Play of colours

The colour in some minerals is really a play of colours like that seen in an oil film or soap bubble. This may be produced when the light is affected by the physical structure of the crystals, such as twinning (p. 21) or cleavage planes (p. 15), or by the development during growth of thin films. Microscopic intergrowths of plate-like inclusions (p. 21) also cause similar light interference.

SALT
A space in the atomic structure of a crystal, caused by a missing atom, can form a colour centre. Coloration of common salt is thought to be caused by this.

HEMATITE
The play of colours on the surface of these hematite crystals from Elba is called iridescence. It is due to the interference of light in thin surface films.

LABRADORITE
The feldspar mineral labradorite can occur as yellowish crystals but more often it forms dull grey crystalline masses. Internal twinning causes interference of light which gives the mineral a sheen, or schiller, with patches of different colours.

Identification

"WHAT IS IT?" This is the first question to ask about a mineral, crystal, or gemstone. In order to identify a crystal it is necessary to test its properties. Most minerals have fixed or well-defined chemical compositions and a clearly identifiable crystal structure (pp. 14–15). These give the mineral a characteristic set of physical properties. Colour (pp. 16–17), habit (pp. 22–23), cleavage (p. 15), and surface features can be studied using a hand lens, but in most cases this is not enough for positive identification. Other properties such as hardness and specific gravity (SG) can be studied using basic equipment, but sophisticated instruments are needed to investigate optical properties, atomic structure, and chemical composition fully.

SPOT THE DIFFERENCE
These two gemstones look almost identical in colour, yet they are two different minerals: a yellow topaz (*left*), and a citrine (*right*).

Sherlock Holmes, the fictitious master of criminal investigation and identification, looks for vital clues with the help of a hound

SEEING DOUBLE
An important property of some crystals is birefringence, or double refraction, as in this rhomb of calcite. Light travelling through the rhomb is split into two rays causing a doubled image.

Doubled image of wool seen through calcite

Chemical beam balance being used to determine specific gravity

Orthoclase SG = 2.6   Galena SG = 7.4

WEIGHING IT UP
Specific gravity is a fundamental property. It is defined as the ratio of the weight of a substance compared to that of an equal volume of water. If W1 = weight of specimen in air, and W2 = its weight in water, then W1 divided by W1-W2 = SG. The two crystals shown are of similar size but their SG differs considerably. This reflects the way the atoms are packed together.

Hardness

The property of hardness is dependent upon the strength of the forces holding atoms together in a solid. A scale of hardness on which all minerals can be placed was devised by F. Mohs in 1812. He selected 10 minerals as standards and arranged them in order of hardness so that one mineral could scratch only those below it on the scale. Intervals of hardness between the standard minerals are roughly equal except for that between corundum (9) and diamond (10).

1 Talc

2 Gypsum

3 Calcite

4 Fluorite

PROBING ABOUT
A modern technique called electron probe micro-analysis was used to investigate the specimen (left). In a scanning electron microscope (SEM) equipped with a special analysis system, a beam of electrons was focussed on the specimen, producing a characteristic x-ray spectrum (below).

10
Diamond

The x-ray spectrum showing large peaks for iron (Fe), arsenic (As), calcium (Ca), and zinc (Zn)

MISTAKEN IDENTITY
It is always important to know the chemical composition of a crystal or mineral, and modern techniques can reveal some surprising results. These small blue-grey crystals on limonite were shown by x-ray methods to be the mineral symplesite (hydrated iron arsenate). However, further analysis showed that they unexpectedly contain some calcium and zinc as well.

Ruby coloured by chromium

Almandine garnet coloured by iron

ABSORBED IN STONE
A spectroscope is often used to distinguish between gemstones of a similar colour. Light enters through a slit and separates into its spectrum of colours (p. 16). If a gemstone is put between the light source and the slit, dark bands appear in the spectrum, where wavelengths have been absorbed by the stone.

SHADOW PLAY
Refractive index (RI) is a mineral's refracting ability, that is its ability to bend a beam of light, and is useful in identification. It can be measured, along with birefringence, with a refractometer. A light is made to pass through the stone, and one or two shadow edges, depending on whether the gem is singly or doubly refractive, form on a scale. The position of the shadow gives the RI.

Spinel
RI: 1.71

Tourmaline
RI: 1.62 and 1.64

9
Corundum

Diamond

Sapphire

8
Topaz

7
Quartz

Chrysoberyl

Topaz

5
Apatite

6
Orthoclase

Opal

Peridot

Amethyst

Garnet

MOHS (1773-1839)
Friedrich Mohs was Professor of Mineralogy at Graz, and later Vienna, Austria. Whilst at Graz he developed the scale of hardness.

Natural growth

CRYSTALS GROW as atoms arrange themselves, layer by layer, in a regular, three-dimensional network (pp. 14–15). They can form from a gas, liquid, or solid and usually start growing from a centre or from a surface. Growth continues by the addition of similar material to the outer surfaces until the supply stops. It is rare to find a perfect crystal. Temperature, pressure, chemical conditions, and the amount of space all affect growth. It is estimated that in an hour, millions and millions of atoms arrange themselves layer by layer across a crystal face. With this number it is not surprising that defects occur.

TWISTED ROUND
Crystals can be bent or twisted like this stibnite. This may be because they were mechanically bent during growth.

CRYSTAL LAYERS
This magnified image, called a photomicrograph, shows the layers of different crystals in a thin section of magmatic rock.

Sal ammoniac crystals

MINERAL SPRINGS
Hot watery solutions and gases containing minerals, such as sal ammoniac (ammonium chloride), sometimes reach the Earth's surface through hot springs, or gas vents known as fumaroles. Here, the minerals may crystallize.

IN THE POCKET
Holes in rocks often provide space in which crystals can grow. Cavities containing fine gem-quality crystals are known as gem pockets. This gem pocket at Mt. Mica, Maine, USA, was discovered in 1979.

SETTLING DOWN
As magma cools, so crystals of various minerals form. Some magmatic rock forms in layers, as different rock-forming minerals settle and crystallize at different times.

CHANGED BY FORCE
As a result of the high temperatures and pressures deep within the Earth's crust, minerals in solid rock can recrystallize, and new minerals form. This process is known as metamorphism. The blue kyanite and brown staurolite crystals in this specimen have been formed in this way.

Quartz

Siderite

Chalcopyrite

TAKING SHAPE
Many minerals crystallize from watery solutions. We only see the final product but can often work out a sequence of events. In this specimen, a fluorite crystal grew first, and was coated with siderite. The fluorite was later dissolved and removed but the coating of siderite kept the characteristic cubic shape of the fluorite crystal. Lastly, crystals of chalcopyrite and quartz grew inside the hollow cube.

BUILDING BLOCKS
Skyscrapers are built in a similar way to crystals – by adding layer upon layer to the same symmetrical shape.

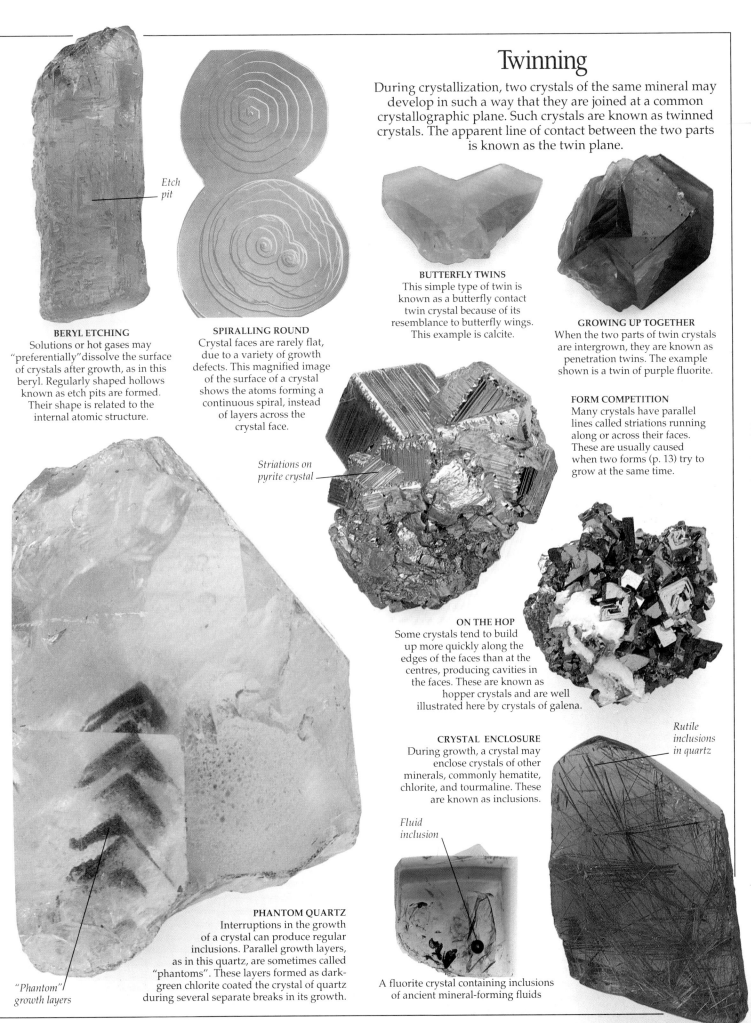

Twinning

During crystallization, two crystals of the same mineral may develop in such a way that they are joined at a common crystallographic plane. Such crystals are known as twinned crystals. The apparent line of contact between the two parts is known as the twin plane.

Etch pit

BERYL ETCHING
Solutions or hot gases may "preferentially" dissolve the surface of crystals after growth, as in this beryl. Regularly shaped hollows known as etch pits are formed. Their shape is related to the internal atomic structure.

SPIRALLING ROUND
Crystal faces are rarely flat, due to a variety of growth defects. This magnified image of the surface of a crystal shows the atoms forming a continuous spiral, instead of layers across the crystal face.

BUTTERFLY TWINS
This simple type of twin is known as a butterfly contact twin crystal because of its resemblance to butterfly wings. This example is calcite.

GROWING UP TOGETHER
When the two parts of twin crystals are intergrown, they are known as penetration twins. The example shown is a twin of purple fluorite.

FORM COMPETITION
Many crystals have parallel lines called striations running along or across their faces. These are usually caused when two forms (p. 13) try to grow at the same time.

Striations on pyrite crystal

ON THE HOP
Some crystals tend to build up more quickly along the edges of the faces than at the centres, producing cavities in the faces. These are known as hopper crystals and are well illustrated here by crystals of galena.

CRYSTAL ENCLOSURE
During growth, a crystal may enclose crystals of other minerals, commonly hematite, chlorite, and tourmaline. These are known as inclusions.

Rutile inclusions in quartz

Fluid inclusion

PHANTOM QUARTZ
Interruptions in the growth of a crystal can produce regular inclusions. Parallel growth layers, as in this quartz, are sometimes called "phantoms". These layers formed as dark-green chlorite coated the crystal of quartz during several separate breaks in its growth.

"Phantom" growth layers

A fluorite crystal containing inclusions of ancient mineral-forming fluids

Good habits

THE GENERAL SHAPE of crystals is called their habit and this is an important part of crystallography. Crystal habit is useful in identification and in well-formed crystals may be so characteristic of a particular mineral that no other feature is needed to identify it. The forms (p. 13) or group of forms that are developed by an individual crystal are often what give it a particular habit. As crystals grow, some faces develop more than others, and it is their relative sizes that create different shapes. Most minerals tend to occur in groups of many crystals rather than as single crystals and rarely show fine crystal shapes. These are called aggregates.

TABULAR
This large red crystal of wulfenite comes from the Red Cloud mine, Arizona, USA. Its habit is known as tabular. Such crystals are often extremely thin. Wulfenite belongs to the tetragonal crystal system.

TWO FORMS
These "mushrooms" are calcite crystals. They show the development of two forms: a scalenohedron forms the "stem", terminated by rhombohedra in parallel position. This group comes from Cumbria, England.

ACICULAR
Looking rather like a sea urchin, the radiating slender mesolite crystals in this aggregate are described as acicular, meaning needle-like. They are very fragile and, like needles, can pierce your skin. This group comes from Bombay, India.

STALACTITIC
The black, lustrous aggregates of goethite in this group are described as stalactitic. The group comes from Coblenz, Rhineland, Germany. Goethite is of the orthorhombic crystal system. It is an important iron ore.

MASSIVE
Crystals which grow in a mass, in which individual crystals cannot be clearly seen, are described as massive. Dumortierite is a rare mineral which is usually massive like this piece from Bahia, Brazil.

CRYSTAL-SHAPED
The Giant's Causeway near Portrush in County Antrim, Northern Ireland looks like a collection of hexagonal crystals. However, the phenomenon is not crystal growth but jointing due to contraction as the basalt lava cooled.

PISOLITIC
This polished slab of limestone from Czechoslovakia is described as pisolitic. Pisolites are round pea-sized aggregates of crystals built of concentric layers, in this case of calcium carbonate.

DENDRITIC
The term used to describe the habit of these copper crystals is dendritic, meaning tree-like. They come from Broken Hill, New South Wales, Australia. Copper often forms in hydrothermal deposits (p. 24) filling holes in some basaltic lava flows, but is also found as grains in sandstones.

PRISMATIC
Beryl crystals are mostly found in granite pegmatites (p. 25) and can grow to be very large. Those illustrated are prismatic – they are longer in one direction than the other. They were found in 1930 in a quarry in Maine, USA, and were over 9 m (30 ft) long.

LENTICULAR
Twinned (p. 21) clear crystals of gypsum form the "ears" on this mass of lenticular crystals from Winnipeg, Canada. Lenticular means shaped like a lentil or lens from the Latin *lenticula*, a lens.

Twinned gypsum crystal

Bladed hornblende crystal

Globular calcite crystal aggregate

CORALLOIDAL
Aggregated crystals that look like coral are said to have a coralloidal habit. This mass of pale-green aragonite crystals came from Eisenberg, Styria, Austria.

GLOBULAR
These aggregated crystals of calcite look a bit like scoops of ice cream, and are described as globular, meaning spherical. The other crystals are clear quartz and the group came from Valenciana mine, Guanajuato, Mexico.

BLADED
The prismatic black crystal in this group is a hornblende crystal and an example of a bladed crystal. The buff-coloured crystals are prismatic serandite and the white crystals are analcime. The group was found at Mont St Hilaire, Quebec, Canada.

QUARTZ IN A CAVE
Crystal growth is influenced by the physical and chemical conditions at the time. Many good crystals grow in cavities which can vary in size from small potato stones (p. 7) to huge caves, as shown in this 19th-century impression of a quartz grotto.

Discovery – recovery

19th-century engraving of miners descending the shaft at Wieliczka salt mine, Poland

THE SEARCH FOR MINERAL deposits including metals and gemstones has been taking place since prehistoric times. Some, such as copper, occur in great quantity; others, such as silver, gold, and diamond are found in much smaller quantities but fetch higher prices. If mining is to be profitable, large quantities of the mineral must occur in one area and be relatively easy to extract, either by surface quarrying, panning and dredging, or if necessary by deep mining. Minerals from which useful metals such as copper, iron, and tin are extracted are called ores.

Chalcopyrite

SCATTERED GRAINS
Rocks of less than one per cent ore are worked today by open-pit quarrying. The ore, such as this chalcopyrite copper ore, occurs as small grains scattered through the rock body. The whole rock has to be worked, a huge amount of gangue, or waste, is produced, and an enormous hole is left.

Copper ore

Quartz

RICH VEIN
Larger concentrations of ore occur in veins, but most high-grade ores have been found and in many cases worked out. Ores in veins are usually worked by deep mining. This vein in altered granite contains chalcopyrite and quartz.

ROMANS IN CORNWALL
The Romans knew of the rich tin deposits in Cornwall, England. Mining techniques have improved since then, but the ore still has to be crushed and separated from the gangue minerals and then refined.

Ingot of refined Cornish tin, produced in 1860

Blue crystals of liroconite, a copper arsenate, from a secondary-enriched layer

Vein of covelline, a copper sulphide, from a secondary sulphide enrichment layer

GRADUAL IMPROVEMENT
The natural process of secondary alteration and enrichment can improve relatively low grade ores to higher concentrations. Groundwaters filter down through the upper layers of rock and carry elements downwards. These are redeposited in lower layers which are thus enriched. Enriched layers in copper deposits may contain azurite, malachite, and sometimes liroconite, or sulphide minerals such as bornite, chalcocite, and covelline.

SWIRLING WATERS
Panning is a simple method of separating minerals. Light gangue minerals are washed away by the swirling action of water in a metal or wood pan, leaving the wanted minerals behind. This technique is often used to sort out gem-rich river gravels in areas such as Myanmar (formerly Burma) and Thailand.

Panning for gold in the Irrawaddy River, Myanmar. The prospector looks for the glint of gold grains within the waste.

Tourmaline crystal

LAST TO GO
Granite pegmatites characteristically consist of large crystals and are the source of many fine gems, including tourmaline (p. 43), topaz (p. 42), and beryl (pp. 38–39). They are formed by the crystallization of the last fluids left after most of the granite has solidified.

DOWN UNDER
Much mining activity takes place underground. This is the Coober Pedy opal mine in South Australia – a source of fine white opals (pp. 40–41).

SMALLER THAN SOME
These beryl crystals measure about 20 x 14 cm (4 x 5 in) but are small compared to some crystals found in pegmatites.

ON THE SURFACE
The Argyle mine in Western Australia is the largest diamond producer in the world. The diamonds are mined by surface-quarrying.

Growing from seed

Scientists have tried to make crystals like those found in the Earth's crust for well over a century. Natural crystals often contain impurities or are flawed in some way (pp. 20–21), but synthetic ones can be made flawless. They can also be made to grow a particular shape and size for specific needs. In recent times a range of artificial crystals have become important to modern technology. Grown crystals are built into almost every electronic or optical device made today. The need for a huge amount of perfect crystals has led to more and more synthetic crystals being made, and it could be said that future developments in electronics will depend on the development of crystal growing techniques.

MELT DOWN
Natural bismuth does occur, but artificial crystal groups, such as this one, are often produced by melting the metal in a crucible and cooling. It is used in solders, electric fuses, and pigments.

IN A FLUX
Many emeralds are produced by the flux fusion technique. A powder made of the components of emerald is heated in a crucible with a solid known as a flux. The flux melts, the powder dissolves, and the mixture is left to cool and form crystals. This method is extremely slow. It takes several months for a crystal to grow.

Cut synthetic emerald

Synthetic emerald crystal

VOYAGE OF DISCOVERY
Crystal growing is important enough for experiments to be done in space. Here, astronaut George Nelson is photographing a protein-crystal-growth experiment on board the space shuttle *Discovery* in 1988.

DRAWN OUT
Pure silicon does not occur naturally so crystals are made artificially for a variety of uses (p. 28). Quartz sand is heated in a crucible with coke to produce nearly pure silicon. In one process a seed crystal on the end of a rotating rod is dipped into the melt and slowly removed, "drawing a crystal".

Melt technique

Excellent crystals may be grown by slow cooling or evaporation of a supersaturated solution (no more will dissolve) of a salt such as halite, alum, or ammonium dihydrogen phosphate (ADP). In the experiment shown, powdered ADP containing a small chrome-alum impurity has been completely dissolved in boiling water and then cooled.

The liquid cools rapidly. Stubby, but cloudy prismatic crystals form.

The crystals grow more slowly, allowing them to become clearer.

At room temperature, crystals still grow slowly due to evaporation.

Cooling stops, but evaporation continues. The crystals slowly grow.

FIRE BOULES

The flame fusion technique was perfected by August Verneuil in about 1900. It is used to make spinel, rutile, and corundum. Powdered material is fed through a flame to fuse into liquid drops which drip on to a support. By gradually pulling the support from the heat, a single crystal, or boule, is formed.

Support for growing crystal

Synthetic sapphire boule

HENRI MOISSON (1852-1907)

Henri Moisson tried to produce artificial diamonds in iron crucibles at the Edison workshops in Paris, France.

EUREKA!

In 1970, the General Electric Company USA announced the laboratory creation of gem-quality diamonds, two of which are shown here.

Synthetic rubies produced in a crucible

Two halves of synthetic ruby boule

GROWN IN SIZE

The French chemist Fremy was the first to grow gem-quality crystals of a reasonable size, in 1877. He discovered a method of making rubies by melting the relevant materials together and fusing them in a porcelain crucible at very high temperatures.

1890 crucible containing a mass of small gemstones

ABRASIVE CHARACTER

The artificial material carborundum (silicon carbide) is produced in electrically fired furnaces with a charge of coke and sand. It is nearly as hard as diamond – 9.5 on Mohs' hardness scale (pp. 18–19) – and is therefore mostly used as an abrasive.

Hexagonal carborundum crystal

GOLD FEVER

Many people over the centuries have tried to find a way to change base metals into gold. A wide range of apparatus must have been needed, if this detail of *The Alchemist at Work* by David Teniers (1582-1649) is anything to go by.

Crystals at work

CRYSTALS PLAY AN IMPORTANT PART in this age of rapid technological and social change. Although the basic understanding of crystals was developed before the 20th century, it is only in the latter part of this century that crystal technology has become so important. Crystals are now used in control circuits, machines, electronics, communications, industrial tools and medicine. We even sometimes use crystals when shopping – in credit cards. From the crystal laboratory (pp. 26–27) has come the silicon chip, ruby laser rods, and the many forms of diamonds for tools. New crystals are continually being developed for specific purposes.

DIAMOND WINDOW
The properties of diamond has led to it being used in space where it has to withstand extreme conditions. Diamond was used in this window for an infrared radiometer experiment on the Pioneer Venus probe. It had to withstand a temperature of 450°C (840°F) near the surface of the planet Venus.

Silicon wafer

SILICON SLICE
Silicon chips are made from very thin slices called "wafers" cut from artificial crystals of pure silicon (p. 26). The wafers are etched with electronic circuits, one for each chip. The circuit patterns are transferred on to a wafer from a piece of film called a matrix.

Silicon chip matrix

CIRCUIT BOARD
Many different chips are needed in a large computer. Each chip has a different circuit and runs a different part of the computer. They are protected in individual cases then connected to the others on a circuit board.

SMART CARDS
There is a tiny built-in mini computer on a silicon chip in each of these "smart cards". Smart cards are still being developed but some are already in limited use. It is expected that in the near future people will be able to use them to store and update personal information, such as the state of their bank account, as well as to make payments.

RUBY ROD
Synthetic ruby crystals are used in some lasers. The heated atoms in the ruby are stimulated by light of a certain wavelength (p. 15) and emit radiation waves in step with the stimulating light. This makes a beam of pure red laser light.

Location of silicon chip

LASERS
This scientist is experimenting with laser beams. Laser beams can be focused to very small points generating intense heat. This is put to use in welding, drilling, and surgery.

Diamond tools

Diamonds are used in a vast number of jobs mainly because they are so hard. They are used in sawing, drilling, grinding, and polishing – from quarrying stone to delicate eye surgery – and come in a large range of sizes, shapes, and strengths. Natural and synthetic diamonds are used, but more than 80 per cent of industrial diamonds are synthetic.

A surgeon using a diamond-bladed scalpel in delicate eye surgery

DRILL BITS
Diamond-tipped drill bits are used for drilling all types of rock. They are used for drilling oil wells and in prospecting for metals and minerals. Some bits contain diamonds set in the surface. The diamonds are different shapes for different purposes. Other bits are impregnated with tiny pieces of diamond grit, or abrasive.

Drill bit containing surface-set natural diamonds

Drill bit impregnated with synthetic diamond abrasive

DIAMOND SCALPEL
As well as being hard, diamond does not corrode. This property is one reason why diamonds are used in surgery. This surgical scalpel contains a blade made from a natural diamond.

Diamond blade

DIAMOND WIRE
Cutting with a diamond wire keeps the loss of material to a minimum. Wires can be used for cutting blocks of stone from quarries as well as for controlled demolition of concrete buildings. The wire can be used around a drum or as a continuous loop.

DIAMOND GRIT
Grit and powders are made from synthetic diamonds or poor-quality natural stones. They are used for polishing and grinding.

"Bead" containing synthetic diamond abrasive

Cutting segment containing synthetic diamond abrasive

SAW BLADE
Saws set with diamonds are used for cutting glass, ceramics, and rocks. The blades have a rim of industrial diamonds in a "carrier" such as brass. This rim is bonded to a steel disc. As the blade cuts, the carrier wears away rapidly and exposes new diamonds.

Cutting an opening for a window in brickwork using a diamond saw

Good vibrations

QUARTZ IS ONE OF THE MOST COMMON MINERALS in the Earth's crust. It is widely distributed as veins (p. 24) and is associated with major mineral deposits. It is one of the chief constituents of granite and is also the main component of sand and sandstones. As quartzite and sandstone, it is used extensively for building and in the manufacture of glass and ceramics. One of the most interesting properties of quartz crystals is piezoelectricity. This can be used to measure pressure, and quartz crystal oscillators provide fixed, very stable frequency control in radios and televisions. The piezoelectric effect of crystals is also used in gas igniters. When a crystal is "squeezed", an electric charge is produced as a spark which lights the gas. Because of its common crystal perfection, quartz is also used in crystal healing.

PAST FAVOURITE
Quartz crystals from Brazil were important material for electronics before synthetic crystals were grown (pp. 26–27). Large quartz crystals are still found there, as demonstrated by this local miner, or *garimpeiro*.

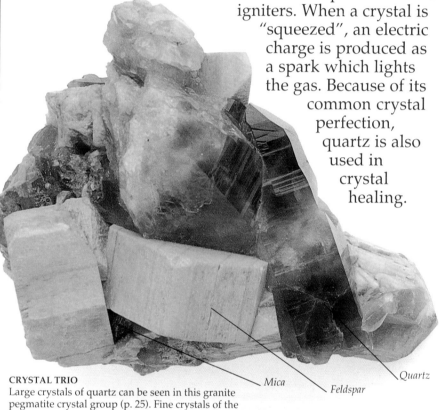

WAVES OF ENERGY
Quartz crystals are used in electronics. They can change a mechanical force, such as a blow from a hammer, into electrical energy, shown here as a wave-form on an oscilloscope screen.

CRYSTAL TRIO
Large crystals of quartz can be seen in this granite pegmatite crystal group (p. 25). Fine crystals of the other two major constituents of granitic rocks, feldspar and mica, are also here.

Mica

Feldspar

Quartz

ENGLISH PRISM
Quartz commonly crystallizes as 6-sided prisms with rhombohedral termination (pp. 12–13). The prism axis shows only threefold symmetry. On many crystals, alternate faces show different growth patterns. This crystal group comes from Cornwall, England.

Hexagonal, prismatic crystal

Quartz

Gold

GOING FOR GOLD
Many quartz veins carry metallic mineral deposits (p. 24). This specimen contains gold. It comes from St David's mine, Gwynedd, Wales, an area famous for the extraction of British gold. The quartz and gold were both deposited by hydrothermal (hot, watery) fluids. In mining practice, the quartz would be considered a "gangue", or unwanted mineral.

Small face showing left-handedness

Right-handed quartz crystal

Left-handed quartz crystal

AMBIDEXTROUS
In a quartz crystal, silicon and oxygen atoms are joined in the shape of a tetrahedron (a four-sided triangular pyramid). These tetrahedra are connected in a spiral arrangement, rather like a spiral staircase and can be left- or right-handed. It is this structure which accounts for the piezoelectricity of quartz.

Crystal pendant thought by some to help with healing

Crystal healing

The laying on of stones is an ancient art. It is thought that as light reflects off the crystals and stones, the electro-magnetic field of the body, the aura, absorbs energy. The receiver can then become aware of mental and emotional causes of physical disease, and heal.

CRYSTAL CLEAR
Rock crystals from groups such as this one from Arkansas, USA are highly prized for their beauty and clarity and are often used for crystal healing.

ALPINE ARCHITECTURE
This "twisted" group of smoky quartz crystals shows some beautiful crystal "architecture". Such crystal groups are often found in the Alps in Europe, where they are known as gwindel.

HEALING POWER
Katrina Raphaell, shown here performing a crystal healing, is the founder of the Crystal Academy in Taos, New Mexico, USA. She has placed stones and crystals upon vital nerve points of the body.

Piezoelectricity

Piezoelectricity was discovered by the brothers Pierre and Jacques Curie in 1880. They discovered that pressure on a quartz crystal causes positive and negative charges to be produced across the crystal. It was later found that an alternating electrical charge placed on a piezoelectric crystal could cause the crystal to vibrate. This is the basis of the use of quartz as oscillator plates to control radio waves, or to keep time.

Jacques and Pierre Curie with their parents

PURE NECESSITY
To meet the demand for pure, flawless quartz crystals necessary for making oscillator plates, synthetic crystals like this one are now grown by a hydrothermal process (p. 26).

WATCH PIECE
This micro-thin quartz crystal slice is used to keep time in a quartz watch. The photograph is greatly enlarged.

Quartz crystal slice

SPLIT-SECOND TIMING
The crystal slice in a quartz watch vibrates more than 30,000 times each second. It is this regularity of vibration which makes it a good timekeeper.

Quartz

QUARTZ IS SILICON DIOXIDE. It occurs as individual crystals and fine-grained masses in a large variety of forms, patterns, and colours. If conditions are right, giant crystals can grow, Brazil being famous for these. The largest recorded rock crystal was about 6 m (20 ft) long and weighed more than 48 tonnes. Other sources of fine quartz include the Swiss Alps, USA, and Madagascar. Quartz is tough and has no cleavage (p. 15) making it ideal for carving and cutting and it is widely used as a gemstone. The name quartz usually refers to individual crystals or coarse-grained aggregates while the fine-grained materials are called chalcedonies or jaspers.

QUARTZ CRYSTAL
Crystal system: trigonal; hardness: 7; specific gravity: 2.65.

DUNES AND DUST
As quartz is relatively hard and common, it forms the major part of sand and also of dust in the air. Dust can therefore damage gems of 6 or less on Mohs' hardness scale (pp. 18–19).

Single crystals

The best-known single crystals of quartz are colourless rock crystal, purple amethyst, rose quartz, smoky quartz, and yellow citrine. These transparent crystals often occur in large enough pieces to be cut as gemstones.

AMETHYST
The most highly prized form of quartz is amethyst. The best comes from two kinds of source. In the Ural Mountains in the USSR crystals occur in veins in granite. In Brazil, Uruguay, and India crystals of superb colour are often found in cavities in basalt.

BACCHUS **BY CARAVAGGIO**
A 16th-century French verse tells how Bacchus, the god of wine, declares in a rage that the first person he passes will be eaten by tigers. This turns out to be a beautiful maiden called Amethyst. The goddess Diana quickly turns Amethyst into a white stone to save her from the tigers. Regretting his anger, Bacchus pours red wine over the stone as an offering to Diana, so turning the stone purple.

ROSE QUARTZ
Single rose quartz crystals are very rare and most rose quartz is massive. It is best cut as cabochons (p. 59) or used for carvings and beads. Some material can be polished to display a star.

Garnet — Pearl — Aquamarine — Agate — Amethyst — Agate — Amazonite

RARE BEAUTY
This 19th-century gold box is set with a superb rare citrine surrounded by a garnet (p. 44), an amazonite, two pearls (p. 55), two aquamarines (p. 39), three agates, and three amethysts.

IMPURE OF HEART
Colourless rock crystal is the purest form of quartz, the many other colours being caused by impurities. Amethyst and citrine contain iron, rose quartz contains titanium and iron, and smoky quartz contains aluminium.

Massive

There are several massive varieties of quartz which are composed of very tiny grains or fibres. Chalcedony – such as carnelian, chrysoprase, and agate – and jasper are distinguished by the different arrangements of these grains. Tiger's-eye and hawk's-eye form when tiny fibres of asbestos are replaced by quartz and iron oxides.

AGATE
The quartz grains in chalcedony are arranged in layers and their build up is clearly visible in the different coloured layers of agate. In this specimen they crystallized progressively towards the middle of a cavity in lava.

Entry point of quartz solution into lava cavity

Bands of agate

TIGER'S-EYE
Originally this vein of tiger's-eye contained silky, blue crystals of asbestos. These were dissolved by solutions which deposited quartz and iron oxides in their place. The structure of the tiny fibres of asbestos was exactly reproduced by the quartz and this gives rise to the light reflection or the "eye".

Polished tiger's-eye showing the eye effect called chatoyancy

A tiger shows why tiger's-eye is so named

Vein of carnelian

Rock crystal

CARNELIAN
Carnelian is the name given to translucent orange-red chalcedony. Most specimens are the result of heat-treating a less attractive chalcedony. The treatment turns iron-bearing minerals into iron oxides which give the more desirable orange-red colours.

JASPER
The interlocking quartz crystals in jasper are arranged in a random mass. They are mixed with colourful impurities making the stone opaque.

CHRYSOPRASE
At its finest, chrysoprase is a vibrant green and the most valuable of the chalcedonies. It has been used in ornament and decorative patterns since prehistoric times. A recent source of some of the best material is Queensland, Australia.

Chrysoprase cameo set in gold

Diamond

DIAMOND CRYSTAL
Crystal system: cubic; hardness: 10; specific gravity: 3.5.

T HE NAME DIAMOND is derived from the Greek word *adamas* meaning "unconquerable", given to the stone because of its supreme hardness. Diamond is made of pure carbon and has an immensely strong crystal structure (p. 14). It is this which makes it the hardest of all minerals. Evidence suggests that diamonds were formed up to 200 km (125 miles) deep within the Earth, and some stones may be as much as 3,000 million years old. Diamonds were first discovered over 2,000 years ago and came mainly from river gravels in India. In 1725, they were found in Brazil which was then the major source until production in South Africa became significant in 1870. Today, about 20 countries produce diamonds. The top producer is Australia, which supplies a quarter of the world's needs, especially for industrial purposes (p. 29). Diamond has great lustre and fire, properties which are best revealed in the brilliant cut (p. 58).

Diamond

VOLCANIC GEMSTONE
This diamond embedded in kimberlite is from South Africa. Kimberlite is a volcanic rock that was first discovered in the Kimberley region of South Africa.

ROUGH DIAMONDS
Rough diamonds mined from kimberlites often have lustrous crystal faces while those recovered from gravels can be quite dull. This is because they may have been carried long distances in rough water with other rocks and gravels.

Mined diamonds

Alluvial diamonds

DIAMOND RUSH
In 1925 some very rich alluvial deposits were discovered at Lichtenburg, South Africa. The government decided to allocate claims (areas of land to mine) on the outcome of a race. So, on 20 August, 1926, 10,000 miners lined up and had to race about 200 m (218 yards) to stake their claims.

Diamonds

SPOT THE DIAMONDS
Diamond-bearing gravels are the result of one of nature's sorting processes. Seriously flawed or fractured stones are more likely to be broken up and eroded away, so a high proportion of the diamonds found in gravels are of gem quality.

UNCONQUERABLE BELIEF
Napoleon Bonaparte is depicted here as First Consul wearing a sword set with the Regent diamond. He hoped the diamond would bring him victory in battle, remembering the ancient belief that a diamond made its wearer unconquerable.

RICH MIX
Conglomerate rock is a mixture of different sizes of rounded pebbles and mineral grains which have been deposited from water and cemented together. This specimen from the west coast of South Africa is particularly rich in diamonds.

INDIAN DIAMOND
This rough diamond is embedded in a sandy conglomerate found near Hyderabad in India. This area was the source of many famous large diamonds such as the Koh-i-noor and the Regent.

VALLEY OF DIAMONDS
Sindbad was once stranded in the legendary Valley of Diamonds. On the valley floor were diamonds guarded by snakes. Sindbad escaped by tying himself to meat thrown down by a diamond collector. As intended by the collector, a bird carried the meat out of the valley stuck with diamonds – and Sindbad!

BUTTERFLY BROOCH
This butterfly brooch is set with over 150 diamonds.

A GIRL'S BEST FRIEND
"Diamonds are a Girl's Best Friend" is the title of a song from the film *Gentlemen Prefer Blondes*. Marilyn Monroe starred in the film wearing a yellow diamond called the Moon of Baroda.

MURCHISON SNUFF BOX
This gold box set with diamonds bears a portrait of Tsar Alexander II of Russia. It was presented in 1867 by the Tsar to Sir Roderick Murchison, the second director of the British Geological Survey, in recognition of Sir Roderick's geological work in Russia.

BRILLIANT COLOURS
Most natural diamonds are near-colourless; truly coiourless ones are rare. A few stones are also found of all colours in the spectrum (p. 16) and good-quality ones are known as fancies.

AGNES SOREL (c 1422-1450)
Agnès Sorel, the mistress of the French king Charles VII, was the first commoner in France to break the law made by Louis IX in the 13th century decreeing that only kings and nobles could wear diamonds.

Famous diamonds
Diamonds of exceptional beauty and rarity are highly prized. Some have long, recorded histories while others have inspired fantastic legends. Most belong to the rich and famous.

THE JEWEL IN THE CROWN
The Koh-i-noor, (mountain of light), is claimed to be the oldest large diamond. It was probably found in India and after belonging to Mughal kings was presented to Queen Victoria in 1850. Its cut, shown in this replica, was unimpressive, so it was recut (p. 58). Today, it is in the British Crown Jewels.

PREMIER DIAMOND
In 1905 the Cullinan crystal was found in the Premier diamond mine in the Transvaal, South Africa. It weighed 3,106 carats and is still the largest diamond ever found. This replica shows its actual size. In 1908 it was cut into 9 large and 96 lesser stones. The two largest, Cullinan I and II, are in the British Crown Jewels (p. 46).

BLUE HOPE
The Hope has a reputation of bringing bad luck, but the sinister stories are untrue. It is 45.52 carats and is now in the Smithsonian Institution, USA.

Corundum

CORUNDUM
Crystal system: trigonal; hardness: 9; specific gravity: 3.96–4.05.

Twin sapphire crystals

Ruby AND SAPPHIRE are varieties of the mineral corundum, an aluminium oxide. Only true red stones are called rubies and the term sapphire on its own indicates a blue stone. Other colours are described as sapphire e.g. yellow sapphire and pink sapphire. Corundum is next to diamond in hardness, so gem crystals are resistant to wear. It is pleochroic, which means the colour of a stone varies when it is viewed in different directions. Most gem crystals are recovered from gravels, and the most famous sources are Myanmar, Kashmir, and Sri Lanka. Today, Australia is the largest producer of blue and golden sapphires. Other producers include Thailand and countries in East Africa.

SOURCE REVEALED
A famous source of fine sapphires is in a valley in the Zanskar range of the Himalayas in Kashmir. It is said that this was only revealed after a landslip in about 1881.

KASHMIR BLUE
Kashmir has a reputation for producing sapphires of the finest blue, like these two examples. The term Kashmir-blue is often used to describe sapphires of this colour from other parts of the world.

Sapphire intergrown with tourmaline

RUSKIN'S RUBY
This Myanmar ruby crystal was presented to the Natural History Museum in London by the philosopher John Ruskin in December 1887. It is about 162 carats. Its deep red colour is the most admired colour for a ruby and is sometimes described as "pigeon's blood" red.

MYANMAR CRYSTAL
Most of the highest-quality rubies come from the Mogok region in Myanmar and this fine crystal embedded in calcite is a good example. Rubies from Myanmar, Pakistan, and Afghanistan are often found in calcite.

Flattened prism of fine-quality ruby from the Mogok district of upper Myanmar

BAZAAR DEALING
This 1930 photograph shows ruby dealers in a Mogok bazaar. Gem-quality corundum is rare and ruby is the most valuable variety of all. Good-quality stones can fetch even higher prices than diamonds of the same size.

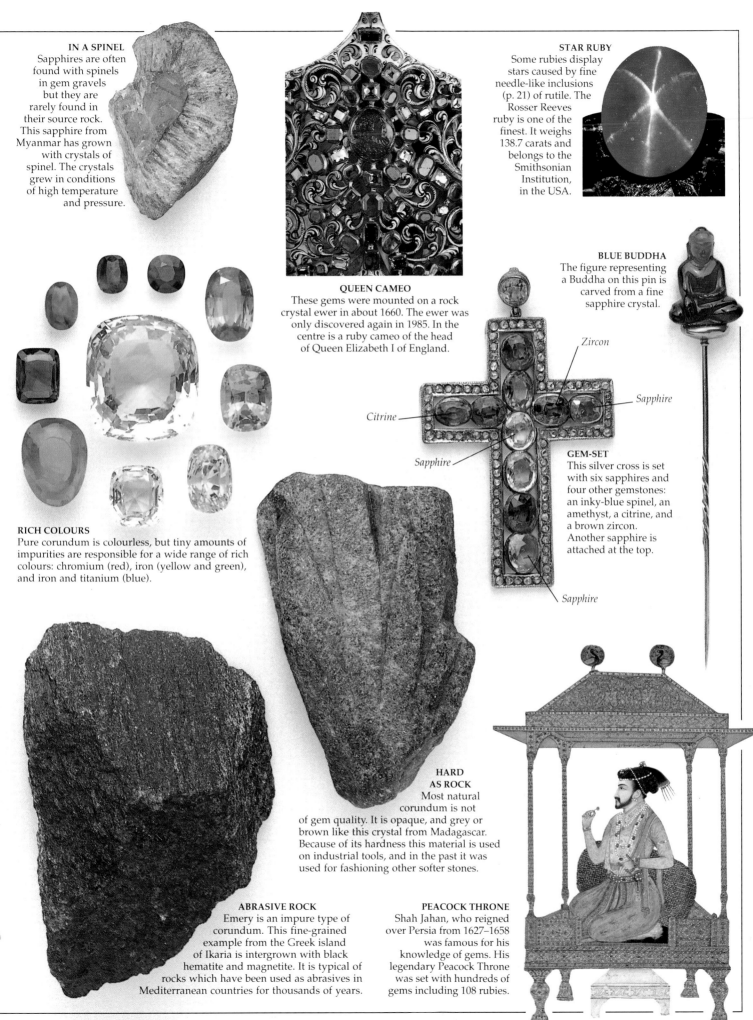

IN A SPINEL
Sapphires are often found with spinels in gem gravels but they are rarely found in their source rock. This sapphire from Myanmar has grown with crystals of spinel. The crystals grew in conditions of high temperature and pressure.

STAR RUBY
Some rubies display stars caused by fine needle-like inclusions (p. 21) of rutile. The Rosser Reeves ruby is one of the finest. It weighs 138.7 carats and belongs to the Smithsonian Institution, in the USA.

QUEEN CAMEO
These gems were mounted on a rock crystal ewer in about 1660. The ewer was only discovered again in 1985. In the centre is a ruby cameo of the head of Queen Elizabeth I of England.

BLUE BUDDHA
The figure representing a Buddha on this pin is carved from a fine sapphire crystal.

Zircon

Citrine

Sapphire

Sapphire

GEM-SET
This silver cross is set with six sapphires and four other gemstones: an inky-blue spinel, an amethyst, a citrine, and a brown zircon. Another sapphire is attached at the top.

Sapphire

RICH COLOURS
Pure corundum is colourless, but tiny amounts of impurities are responsible for a wide range of rich colours: chromium (red), iron (yellow and green), and iron and titanium (blue).

HARD AS ROCK
Most natural corundum is not of gem quality. It is opaque, and grey or brown like this crystal from Madagascar. Because of its hardness this material is used on industrial tools, and in the past it was used for fashioning other softer stones.

ABRASIVE ROCK
Emery is an impure type of corundum. This fine-grained example from the Greek island of Ikaria is intergrown with black hematite and magnetite. It is typical of rocks which have been used as abrasives in Mediterranean countries for thousands of years.

PEACOCK THRONE
Shah Jahan, who reigned over Persia from 1627–1658 was famous for his knowledge of gems. His legendary Peacock Throne was set with hundreds of gems including 108 rubies.

Beryl

BERYLS ARE POPULAR AS GEMS for their fine colours and resistance to wear. The most well-known varieties are emerald (green) and aquamarine (blue green). Yellow beryl is known as heliodor, and pink beryl is morganite. The name beryl can be traced to Greek, Roman, and possibly Sanskrit sources, and it is highly likely that aquamarine and heliodor were known in prehistoric times. Beryl is found in pegmatites (p. 25) and granites and in its massive, opaque, non-gem form can occur in crystals weighing many tonnes. The record holder is a crystal which was found in Madagascar weighing 36 tonnes and measuring about 18 m (60 ft) long.

BERYL CRYSTAL
Crystal system: hexagonal; hardness: 7.5; specific gravity 2.63–2.91.

SOVIET HOST
A typical source of emeralds is mica schist. This kind of source was found in the early 1800s in the Ural mountains, USSR. Many of these crystals have mica and amphibole inclusions (p. 21), the same rock as the host.

SPANISH SPOILS
The Chibcha Indians of Colombia mined emeralds which, through trade, reached the Incas of Peru and the Aztecs of Mexico. They were seen there by the Spanish in the early 1500s who determined to find their source. They did not find the Chivor mine until 1537 and most of the emeralds sent back to the Spanish court were pillaged from the Incas' treasure.

MINED FOR LIFE
The finest emeralds in the world come from around Muzo and Chivor in Colombia. Many are mined and exported illegally and there are often robberies and murders.

An 1870 engraving showing convicts working the Colombian emerald mines

ANCIENT ACCESS
Emeralds were mined near the Red Sea in Egypt from about 1500 B.C. The mines were rediscovered in 1816 by the French adventurer Cailliaud, but attempts at viable mining were not a success. This old entrance to one of Cleopatra's mines was discovered in about 1900.

FINE CUT
This exceptionally fine, 911-carat, cut aquamarine belongs to the Smithsonian Institution in Washington, USA.

SECOND-CLASS CRYSTAL
A few emeralds are still found in Egypt. They come from an area of granite, schist, and serpentine. Most crystals are blueish green with many inclusions and do not compare in quality with the best Colombian emeralds.

COLOUR CAUSES
Pure beryl is colourless. The spectacular reds and pinks are caused by manganese, the blues and yellows by iron. The beautiful emerald green is due to tiny amounts of chromium or vanadium.

SEA GREEN
Aquamarine literally means sea water, which accurately describes its colour. It has a range from pale green to blue, caused by varying amounts of different forms of iron. It is relatively common with sources in many countries but the main source is Brazil.

Morganite

Heliodor

DRY RED
Red beryl is extremely rare and is the only natural beryl that contains no water in its crystal structure. It occurs in "dry" volcanic rocks in the western USA. This fine specimen comes from the Wah Wah Mountains in Utah.

Tourmaline inclusions

TURKISH DELIGHT
The Topkapi Palace Treasury in Istanbul, Turkey, contains many pieces with fine emeralds. The hilt of this 18th-century dagger holds three, plus one cut as a hexagonal slice and hinged over a small watch at the end.

GEM BELTS
This large crystal of beryl is made up of zones of the varieties morganite and heliodor. This gem-quality specimen comes from Brazil, but other sources of these varieties include California, Madagascar, and Pakistan.

Opal

THE POPULARITY OF OPAL has risen and fallen over the centuries. The Ancient Romans used it as a symbol of power but at different times since then, it has been considered to be unlucky. The Aztecs mined opal over 500 years ago in Central America which is still an important source, especially of fire opal. The top producer of black and white opal is Australia where it was first discovered during the 1870s. Opal is one of the few non-crystalline gems. It has a tendency to crack and chip especially due to extreme temperature changes or a hard knock. The exciting flashes of colour shown by precious opal are best displayed in cabochons although Mexican fire opals are usually cut as brilliants or step-cuts (p. 58).

OPAL
Crystal system: amorphous or poorly-crystalline; hardness: 5.5–6.5; specific gravity: 1.98–2.25.

ROMAN SOURCE
This piece of white opal comes from Cervenica, Czechoslovakia, the source used by the Romans. This region was once part of Hungary and the opal from here is usually described as Hungarian.

THE PLAGUE OF VENICE
This detail of a painting by Antonio Zanchi depicts the Black Death of the 14th century. The people in Venice, Italy, noticed that opals became brilliant when a wearer caught the disease and dulled when the person died. This reinforced the belief that opals were unlucky.

FLASH OF LIGHTNING
The finest black opal comes from Lightning Ridge, New South Wales, Australia. Against its dark body the colour flashes are quite dramatic and this attraction, coupled with its greater rarity, makes it more valuable than white opal.

NON-FLASHY
Non-precious opal without flashes of colour is called potch opal. Rose opal is potch but its striking colour has led to it being used in beads and decorative jewellery. This specimen comes from France and there are other sources in Idaho.

AUSTRALIAN FAIR
All the major Australian opal deposits occur in sedimentary rocks in the Great Artesian Basin. Famous mines include White Cliffs, Lightning Ridge, and Coober Pedy. A popular way of marketing the opal is in doublets and triplets (p. 56).

GLASSY LOOK
Clear glassy-looking opal (hyalite) occurs in cavities in volcanic lavas. This example is from Bohemia but there are several other sources. If similar material shows a play of colour it becomes the prized water opal. Another kind of opal called hydrophane is opaque but appears colourless in water.

Greatly enlarged photograph of precious opal, showing the ordered silica spheres in the structure

FLASHING LIGHTS

Precious opal displays flashes of different colours. They depend on the size of the silica spheres in the structure. Opal with a background colour of grey, blue, or black, is called black. Others are called white.

ON THE MAP

"Prospector's brooches", shaped like the map of Australia, were made to mark the arrival on the gemstone market of Australian opal. This one is thought to have been made around 1875.

Opal cameo *Dawn with Cupid and Psyche* now in the Natural History Museum, London

MEXICAN FIRE

Mexico has long been famous for its fire opal. This is a nearly transparent variety, still showing flashes of colour. It ranges from yellow to orange and red.

MOVED IN

The opal localities in Australia are extremely hot so when mines are worked out, those excavations near the surface are adapted to provide relatively cool and pleasant living conditions.

PRECIOUS FOSSIL

Opal often replaces the tissues of wood, and bones and shells of ancient animals, in a kind of fossilization. It grows bit by bit in place of the original material. This piece of wood from Nevada, USA, has been replaced by precious and potch opal.

BEAUTIFUL BOULDER

Boulder opal is hardened sandy clay with variable amounts of iron oxides and layers of precious opal. If enough iron is present, the rock is very dark brown and flat surfaces of opal can be carved into beautiful cameos.

Precious opal   Potch opal

OPAL FRUIT

This was an aggregate of radiating crystals of glauberite. It has been completely replaced by precious opal. This kind of opal is found in Australia and is popularly known as "pineapple opal".

DRUNK AND DRIVING

Opal was given a bad name in the 17th-century court of the French king Louis XIV. He named his coaches after gemstones. The driver of the *Opal* was usually drunk, and the coach was considered unlucky! This is a detail of a picture by Van der Meulen called *Entry into Arras by Louis XIV and Marie Thérèse*.

Other gemstones

THE PROPERTIES OF A GEMSTONE are said to be beauty, rarity, and durability and these criteria have been applied to many species. As well as quartz (pp. 32–33), diamond (pp. 34–35), ruby and sapphire (pp. 36–37), beryl (pp. 38–39), and opal (pp. 40–41), gemstones to be seen in jewellers' shops include topaz, tourmaline, garnet, peridot, and many others. Some species such as kunzite, sphene, and fluorite are too soft or rare to be in general circulation as gemstones and are cut only for collectors on the basis of their beauty and rarity.

MARVELLOUS GEMS
"Fishing for pearls and gathering turquoises" from *The Book of Marvels* by Marco Polo.

Topaz

The mineral we know as topaz was only given the name in the first half of the 18th century. Prior to that its history is not clear. The name topaz is said to come from *Topazius*, the Greek name for Zabargad, an island in the Red Sea. This island is however a source of what we now call peridot (p. 45).

TOPAZ CRYSTAL
Crystal system: orthorhombic; hardness: 8; specific gravity: 3.52–3.56.

CRYSTAL FAME
The most famous source of topaz is Brazil, which is where this pale-blue crystal comes from. It is also found in Mexico, USA, Sri Lanka, Japan, USSR, Nigeria, and Zaire.

Line of cleavage

NEEDS PROTECTION
Although it is very hard, topaz can be broken easily because it has one direction of perfect cleavage (p. 15). A line of cleavage can be seen clearly in this crystal. If used in jewellery, the setting for a topaz must therefore provide protection from accidental knocks.

ONE OF THE BEST
The finest golden topaz crystals come from the Ouro Preto area in Brazil, and this wedge-shaped prism is typical of them. Some may show colour zoning from golden brown to pink. Gems containing a hint of pink are often called imperial topaz.

TOPAZ TRICKS
Like diamond, topaz is commonly found in gravel as rounded waterworn pebbles. It also has a specific gravity very similar to that of diamond and this has led to some premature celebrations.

WATER COLOURS
Topaz is an aluminium silicate containing about 20 per cent water and fluorine. Those crystals with more water than fluorine are golden brown or rarely pink; those with more fluorine than water are blue or colourless.

BRAZILIAN PRINCESS
This topaz was cut in 1977 and weighed 21,327 carats. The largest cut stone today is 36,853 carats.

Tourmaline

Tourmaline is a mineral with a complex chemistry crystallizing as prisms with flat or wedge-shaped terminations. Every crystal has a different structure at each end, sometimes indicated by different colours. This gives tourmaline an unusual electrical property. If a crystal is gently warmed, one end becomes positively charged and the other negatively charged, which is the reason for its tendency to attract dust.

TOURMALINE CRYSTAL
Crystal system: trigonal; hardness: 7–7.5; specific gravity: 3–3.25.

MEDICINE OR MINERAL
The Victorian philosopher John Ruskin, shown here in 1885, wrote "The chemistry of tourmaline is more like a medieval doctor's prescription than the making of a respectable mineral!"

FRAMED UP
This slice across a tourmaline prism shows typical threefold symmetry and a triangular cross-section. The zones of colour illustrate how the crystal was built up in layers, each layer being a different phase of crystallization. The final shape of the crystal is controlled by the last phase which in this case formed a hexagonal "frame".

The growth rings seen in some crystals are similar to those of tree trunks

BLACK AND GREEN
Tourmaline is pleochroic which means it is a different colour when viewed down different axes (pp. 12–13). These green crystals would be almost black if viewed down the long axis.

Tourmaline crystal

CLOSE NEIGHBOURS
This tourmaline is unusual in being attached to its neighbour (quartz) by a prism face. The pink prism crystallized first, then green tourmaline formed the terminations.

SET IN GRANITE
Gem-quality tourmalines are most often found in pegmatite veins (p. 25) or granites. Brazil, USSR, USA, East Africa, and Afghanistan have all produced fine crystals.

Cut stone showing the two colours of "watermelon" tourmaline

MULTI-COLOURED
Tourmaline shows the greatest colour range of any gemstone and some crystals are themselves more than one colour. "Watermelon" tourmaline has pink cores and green outer zones.

Tourmaline crystal

Continued on next page

Continued from previous page

Ring set with
almandine garnet

GARNET CRYSTALS
Crystal system: cubic;
hardness: 6.5–7.5;
specific gravity:
3.52–4.32.

Cut demantoid
garnet

Garnet

Garnet is the name of a family of chemically related minerals
that includes almandine, pyrope, spessartine, grossular, and
andradite. They can all be found as gemstones with the
almandine-pyrope group being the most widely used. Because
of the different chemical compositions, garnet occurs in most
colours other than blue. Sources of gem-quality
material include Czechoslovakia, South
Africa, USA, Australia, Brazil, and Sri Lanka.

Cut
pyrope
garnet

PYROPE
The deep-red garnet, pyrope, was
popular in the 19th century. Most stones
came from Bohemia (Czechoslovakia).

DEMANTOID
Emerald-green
demantoid is the
most prized of all
the garnets. The
finest stones come
from the Ural
mountains in
the USSR.

Spessartine
cabochon

SPESSARTINE
The beautiful orange colours of spessartine are
caused by manganese. Spessartine is not often
seen in jewellery as gem-quality crystals are rare.

FRUITY NAME
"Garnet" may come from *pomum granatum* , Latin for
pomegranate. The gem colour of the almandine-
pyrope group is like that of pomegranate fruit.

ALMANDINE
Garnet commonly crystallizes
as icositetrahedrons, like these
almandine crystals. Almandine
usually has a very deep colour
so it is often cut as cabochons
(p. 59) with the backs
hollowed out to make
it more transparent.

FIT FOR A KING
This fine 7th-century purse lid was among many garnet-set pieces found
in an Anglo-Saxon royal burial ship in Sutton Hoo, Suffolk, England.
The quality of the workmanship of all the pieces indicates the high
status of their owner.

ANDRADITE
Most andradite
garnet does not
occur as gem-quality
crystals. Only green
demantoid, the yellow
variety topazolite, and this
black variety, melanite, are used
as gemstones. Black garnet was
once used as mourning jewellery.

Cut grossular garnets

COLOUR TRACES
Brilliant-green grossular contains trace
amounts of vanadium, while the
yellow and red stones contain iron.The
red variety is known as hessonite.

GROSSULAR
Some grossular
garnet is said to look
like gooseberries and
the name grossular
probably comes from
the Latin for gooseberry –
grossularia. This specimen
of pink grossular from Mexico
clearly shows dodecahedral crystals,
one of the two major habits of garnet.

PERIDOT CRYSTAL
Crystal system: orthorhombic; hardness: 6.5; specific gravity: 3.22–3.40.

Peridot

Peridot is a French word and may derive from the Arabic *faridat* meaning a gem. It is the gem variety of the mineral olivine, a magnesium and iron silicate, which is common in volcanic rocks.

Olivine-rich rock

Lava

Cut peridot from Arizona

Cut peridot from Norway

Cut peridot from Myanmar

PERIDOT SUPPLIERS
The largest peridots come from Zabargad and Myanmar, but Arizona and Hawaii in the USA, and Norway, have also supplied fine gems.

Ring set with peridot

ISLAND GEM
Peridot usually occurs in rocks intergrown with other minerals. The island of Zabargad in the Red Sea is one of the few places in the world where crystals with distinct faces, such as these, are found.

VOLCANIC BOMB
This solidified lava contains fragments of rock rich in olivine. The lava came from deep within the Earth carrying the rock with it and the whole piece was ejected through a volcano as a volcanic bomb.

NAME CHANGE
There have been peridot mines on the island of Zabargad in the Red Sea for a long time. The stones from here were known by the Ancient Greeks as topazos (p. 42).

Moonstone

Moonstone is the best-known feldspar gem. Feldspars are common in rocks, but are rarely of gem quality. There are two main groups: one which is rich in potash and includes the moonstones; one which is rich in soda and calcium and includes sunstone. They range in hardness from 6–6.5 and in specific gravity from 2.56–2.76.

SUNSTONE
The bright spangles in sunstones are reflections from tiny dark-red flakes of hematite. Some are arranged parallel giving extra brightness in some directions.

The Sun and the Moon – appropriate names for these two stones

BLUEISH MOON
Most moonstones are colourless with a silvery or blueish sheen, but some varieties may be steely grey, orange pink, yellow, or pale green. The grey stones particularly may show good cat's-eyes (p. 59).

Pin set with sunstone

MOONSTONE
This large specimen of pegmatitic feldspar from Myanmar shows the moonstone sheen. Pegmatites (p. 25) may also be the source of moonstones sometimes found in the gem gravels of Sri Lanka and India.

Ring set with moonstone

Continued on next page

Spinel

The most beautiful red and blue spinels can rival ruby and sapphire in their richness. Until the 19th century, red spinels were called balas rubies which led to some confusion. The scientist Romé de l'Isle (p. 12) was the first to distinguish clearly between true ruby and red spinel. The term balas may relate to a source of these stones in Balascia, now called Badakhshan, in Afghanistan.

PRINCELY REWARD
The Black Prince, son of King Edward III of England, helped Pedro the Cruel, King of Castille, Spain, to win the Battle of Najera in 1367. He was rewarded with a balas ruby, now in the Imperial State Crown.

SPINEL CRYSTAL
Crystal system: cubic; hardness: 8; specific gravity: 3.5–3.7.

POLISHED OVER
This crystal has been polished to remove surface blemishes but it still has its original octahedral shape.

SMALL DISTORTION
Spinel usually crystallizes as octahedra. This specimen is a crystal aggregate of small distorted octahedra in parallel growth. Spinel often occurs as twins (p. 21) and when flat, such crystals are called macles.

Black Prince's ruby

Cullinan II diamond

REFORMED CHARACTER
This specimen from Lake Baikal, USSR, contains octahedra of blue spinel set in a matrix of white calcite and shiny muscovite mica. Originally it was probably an impure limestone which completely recrystallized under moderate temperature and pressure.

LYING IN STATE
The Black Prince's ruby in the British Imperial State Crown is really a 170-carat spinel, once called a balas ruby. It is mounted above another famous stone, the Cullinan II diamond (p. 35). The Timur ruby, which belongs to Queen Elizabeth II, is also a spinel.

CLOSE TO HOME
Most gem stones are recovered from gravels in Sri Lanka and Myanmar. These Myanmar fragments are not very worn, indicating that they did not travel far.

THORNY CRYSTALS
These beautifully crystallized octahedra from Bodenmais in Germany are gahnite, a zinc-rich variety of spinel. They show the typical triangular-shaped crystal faces of spinel which may account for the possible derivation of its name from the Latin *spina* meaning thorn.

CRYSTAL COLOURS
Pure spinel is colourless. The beautiful reds and pinks are due to small amounts of chromium in the crystals. Blues and greens are caused by iron and, rarely, by zinc.

Zircon

The name zircon comes from the Arabic *zargoon* meaning vermillion or golden coloured. Sri Lanka has been a source of zircons for 2,000 years but today stones also come from Thailand, Australia, and Brazil. Colourless zircon looks like diamond in lustre and fire and is used as a diamond simulant (p. 57), but it is softer and may look "sleepy" due to inclusions and double refraction (p. 19).

The colour of red hyacinths may account for red zircon once being known as hyacinth

NATURAL COLOURS
Zircon is zirconium silicate, colourless when pure, but found in a wide range of colours in nature because of different impurities.

ZIRCON CRYSTAL
Crystal system: tetragonal; hardness 7.5; specific gravity: 4.6–4.7.

RADIO-ACTIVE
This exceptionally large pebble from Sri Lankan gem gravels shows a typical zircon colour. Some zircons contain so much uranium and thorium that the radio-activity of these elements breaks down the crystal structure and the stone becomes amorphous, or non-crystalline.

HEAT-TREATMENT
Colourless, blue, and golden zircons can be produced by heating red-brown crystals. Heating in an oxygen-free atmosphere produces blue zircon; heating in air, i.e. with oxygen, produces a golden colour. Some colourless stones are produced by both methods. These colours may fade but can be restored by reheating.

Natural brown zircon crystals

Heat-treated blue zircon crystals

Stones cut from heat-treated zircon

Chrysoberyl

Gem chrysoberyl is exceeded in hardness only by diamond and corundum. The yellow, green, and brown colours are caused by iron or chromium. There are three varieties: clear yellow-green gems; cat's-eye or cymophane, usually cut as cabochons to display the "eye" effect (p. 59); alexandrite, famous for its dramatic colour change. Sri Lanka and Brazil are sources for all three but the best alexandrites come from the USSR.

ALEXANDRITE
Alexandrite was discovered in the Ural Mountains, USSR, on the birthday of Tzar Alexander II in 1830, hence the name. They appear a deep green in daylight, and red in artificial light, matching the Russian imperial colours.

Cut yellow chrysoberyl

Cut alexandrite

POPULAR IN PORTUGAL
Yellow-green chrysoberyls were found in Brazil in the 18th century. These became very popular in Portuguese and Spanish jewellery.

CHRYSOBERYL CRYSTAL
Crystal system: orthorhombic; hardness: 8.5; specific gravity: 3.68–3.78.

Collectors' items

WITH OVER 3,000 SPECIES of minerals to choose from, the potential number of gems would appear at first to be very large. But crucial factors such as hardness (pp. 18–19), durability, and rarity reduce the number of commercial gems to a few tens. Many people collect rarities that are not in general circulation. They may seek the rare colours or exceptional sizes of common gems, or cut examples of minerals too soft or fragile to wear in jewellery. For example, blende and sphene are available in reasonable quantities but are too soft for constant wear. Benitoite is durable enough to be worn but is too rare to be generally available.

AXINITE
The most beautiful wedge-shaped crystals of brown axinite come from Bourg d'Oisans in France and display flashes of grey and violet in different directions. Although they were once extremely rare, crystals are being recovered more regularly from the Sri Lankan gem gravels.

SPHENE
Ranging from golden yellow brown to bright emerald green, sphene has great lustre and fire but is too soft for general wear. The finest gems come from the Austrian and Swiss Alps, Myanmar, and California, USA.

FRENCH COLLECTION
The first specimens of the major mineral collection in the Museum of Natural History in Paris, France, were brought together in Louis XIII's pharmacy and botanical gardens. This engraving shows it as it was in 1636, seven years before the king died.

ALPINE EXPERTS
Many fine crystals are collected from crystal-lined clefts in the Alps by people known as strahlers. Strahlers are experienced mountaineers but also talented mineral collectors, usually with great knowledge of a particular Alpine area.

TANZANITE
The purplish-blue gem variety of the mineral zoisite is tanzanite. It was found in northern Tanzania in 1967 and is remarkable for its displays of rich blue, magenta, and yellowish grey. Many crystals are greenish grey and are heat treated to the more attractive blue.

CORDIERITE
Fine, gem-quality cordierite comes from Sri Lanka, Myanmar, Madagascar, and India. Cordierite is exceptional in showing very strong pleochroism, from deep purplish blue in one direction, to pale yellowish grey in another. This pleochroism was used by the Vikings for navigating their long boats (p. 60) and has also led to the crystals being called "water sapphires".

DANBURITE
The mineral danburite is named after Danbury, Connecticut, in the USA, where it was first found as colourless crystals in a pegmatite (p. 25). Fine yellow stones come from Madagascar and Myanmar and colourless stones from Japan and Mexico.

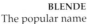

BENITOITE
The colour of benitoite crystals can be compared with that of fine sapphires. They display similar fire to diamonds, but remain collector's stones because of their rarity. Benitoite comes from San Benito County, USA, after which it is named (p. 11).

BLENDE
The popular name for sphalerite, the world's major source of zinc, is blende. Normally it is opaque grey to black, but gem-quality reddish brown, yellow, and green crystals come from Mexico and Spain. The rich colours are very attractive but the stones are too soft to be used in jewellery.

Blende crystals in matrix

Rough blende crystal

The San Benito Mine in 1914 showing the open cut and an ore bucket on the left

Kunzite crystal

Cut pale-green spodumene

Cut kunzite

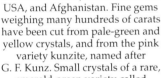

SPODUMENE
Magnificent crystals of spodumene come from Brazil, California in the USA, and Afghanistan. Fine gems weighing many hundreds of carats have been cut from pale-green and yellow crystals, and from the pink variety kunzite, named after G. F. Kunz. Small crystals of a rare, emerald-green variety called hiddenite are found in North Carolina in the USA, and Sri Lanka.

George Frederick Kunz, an author on gems, who worked for the New York jewellers Tiffany's early this century

GOLDNEY GROTTO
Precious stones and corals are amongst items collected to cover the walls and pillars of this underground grotto. It was built between 1737 and 1764 near Bristol, England.

SCAPOLITE
Myanmar and East Africa are sources of scapolite gems. They occur in pastel shades of yellow, pink, purple, and fine cat's-eyes (p. 33).

SINHALITE
Originally traded as peridot from Sri Lanka, sinhalite was proved in 1950 to be a new species. Mineralogists in the British Museum named it after an old name for Sri Lanka – Sinhala.

FIBROLITE
This bluish-violet stone of 19.84 carats is fibrolite, a rare variety of the mineral sillimanite. It comes from Myanmar and is one of the largest in the world. Andalusite has the same chemical composition – aluminium silicate – but a different structure. The gem-quality stones show bold red and green pleochroic colours. Fine examples come from Brazil and Sri Lanka.

Cut fibrolite

Cut andalusite

Stones for carving

MICROCRYSTALLINE ROCKS and minerals have been used in decoration for thousands of years. The best known are the jades, lapis lazuli, and turquoise and there are many more which are suitable for carving work. Ancient civilizations such as the Egyptians, Chinese, and Sumerians used jade, lapis, and turquoise to make jewellery. South American Indians and the Maoris of New Zealand have been carving turquoise and jade for centuries.

TURQUOISE TRADITION
Traditional Indian jewellery has been made for thousands of years in the south-western United States where most turquoise is still produced.

MALACHITE
Malachite is a vivid green copper mineral. It is often found as kidney-shaped masses in bands of colour. It is 4 on the hardness scale (pp. 18–19) and has a specific gravity of 3.8. Zaire, Zambia, Australia, and the Soviet Union are the main sources.

Turquoise

The name turquoise comes from the French *pierre turquoise* meaning stone of Turkey, most of it in the past being sold in Turkey. It occurs in nodules and veins of green or blue. Copper makes it blue; iron makes it green. It has a specific gravity of 2.6–2.9 and a hardness of 5–6.

Lapis lazuli

Lapis lazuli is not a single mineral but a rock consisting of blue lazurite with variable amounts of calcite and pyrite. The best, from Afghanistan, consists mostly of lazurite and is deep blue. It is 5.5 on Mohs' hardness scale and has a specific gravity of 2.7–2.9. There are other sources in the Soviet Union and Chile.

White calcite

PERSIAN BLUE
The name lapis lazuli is derived from the Persian word *lazhward* meaning blue. The blue colour is caused by sulphur which is an essential part of its composition.

NATURAL MOSAIC
Turquoise is rare in large masses and is more often found forming mosaics. The finest blue turquoise comes from Iran (previously called Persia) where it has been used in decoration for almost 6,000 years.

POPULAR JEWEL
Lapis lazuli has been used extensively for beads and other pieces of jewellery.

Blue Persian turquoise engraved and inlaid with gold

MEDIEVAL PAINTING
In medieval times lapis lazuli was crushed and purified to make the paint pigment ultramarine. It was used to paint the Wilton Diptych, a detail of which is shown here. This famous altar piece is now in the National Gallery in London.

ANCIENT SKULL
This mask, shaped around a human skull, was made by the Aztecs, an ancient civilization of Central America. It is made of turquoise and lignum, and may represent Tezcatlipoca, an important Aztec god.

Jade

The Spanish conquerors of Mexico believed that the Indians' green stones would cure kidney ailments. They called them kidney stones or *piedra de hyada* and from this the word jade was derived. In Europe, the name was then given to material of the same colour and hardness which was imported from China. It was only in 1863 that they were proved to be two different minerals now called jadeite and nephrite.

LIFE JACKET
The Ancient Chinese believed that jade had the power to give life and used it to try to preserve the dead. They linked plates of nephrite around the corpse to make a funeral suit. This one belonged to a princess of the 2nd century B.C. and is linked with gold.

JADEITE
The major source of jadeite is Myanmar. It varies widely in colour so a window is cut in stones for sale to show the colour. The most prized colour is the emerald-green jadeite known as imperial jade. Jadeite has a hardness of 6.5–7 and a specific gravity of 3.3–3.5.

Jadeite fashioned into a ball

Nephrite snail designed by the famous Russian jeweller, Fabergé

CHINESE CAMEL
This nephrite camel was carved in China. White and cream nephrites contain very little iron. More iron causes the spinach-green stones of the USSR, Canada, and New Zealand and the black jade of South Australia.

NEPHRITE
Nephrite is made of interlocking grains making the stone tough. The "greenstone" used by the Maoris of New Zealand is nephrite. It has a hardness of 6.5 and a specific gravity of 2.9–3.1.

Other stones

Many other stones are popular for carving, mainly because of their colour. These include malachite, serpentine, blue john, and rhodonite, as well as marbles and alabaster.

SERPENTINE
The patterns in serpentine often look like snake-skin and carvers can use these to create works of art. Some is soft and easy to carve but the yellow-green variety bowenite, a favourite of Chinese carvers, is harder – up to 6 on Mohs' scale.

RHODONITE
The bright pink colour of rhodonite (rhodo meaning pink) is caused by manganese. It has a hardness of about 6 and is used for carving and inlays. Sources of gem material include USSR, Canada, and Australia.

BLUE JOHN
The distinctive purple and pale yellow, banded fluorite called blue john comes from Derbyshire in England. It is fragile so is usually bonded with resins to make it easier to work and harder-wearing.

19th-century blue john vase

Precious metals

GOLD, SILVER, AND PLATINUM are crystalline, although single crystals are rarely found. Gold and silver were among the earliest metals worked, over 5,000 years ago. Platinum was first noted in 1735 as a white metal used by the Chibcha Indians of Colombia and today it is more valuable than gold and silver. All three metals are useful because they are relatively soft and easy to work. They are difficult to destroy and have high SGs (p. 18).

CALIFORNIA GOLD RUSH
The desire for gold has driven people to inhabit areas of the Earth from the frozen Arctic to the scorching desert. Gold seekers rushed to California, USA in 1848 and many became rich. Most of the gold was recovered from placer deposits by panning (p. 25).

WELL PLACED
These are deposits of erosion debris from gold-bearing rock. Small particles of gold can be recovered from placer deposits by washing away the sand and gravel.

Gold

Gold is used as a standard against which wealth is measured. Pure gold is a dense (SG=19.3) but soft (H=2.5–3) metal. Before it can be used, it has to be refined and for most uses it is alloyed with other metals to make it harder. Purity of gold for jewellery is measured in carats, pure gold being 24 carats.

EXCELLENT NUGGET
This fine crystalline gold nugget, is known as the Latrobe nugget. It was found in 1855 in the presence of His Excellency C. J. Latrobe, the Governor of what was then the colony of Victoria, Australia. Large nuggets of gold are rare.

GOLD SANDWICH
Gold is sometimes found concentrated in hydrothermal veins and associated with quartz. A wafer-thin layer of crystalline gold can be seen in this quartz vein from New Zealand.

WORTH ITS WEIGHT
The famous golden Buddha of Bangkok is 5.5 tonnes of solid gold. It is worth over £28 million ($50 million) and is the most valuable religious item in the world.

BUILT ON GOLD
Between 1700 and 1900 the Asante kingdom dominated the area of Africa now known as Ghana. Its power was mostly founded upon its gold resources. Gold dust was the currency for internal trade. This lion ring is from the Asante kingdom.

RARE SIGHT
It is usual for gold to occur as fine grains scattered throughout a rock, or as invisible gold that cannot be seen by the naked eye. This group of crystals from Zimbabwe is therefore extremely rare.

Platinum

Platinum plays a key role in modern technology. It is used as a standard weight, for surgical instruments, and of course in jewellery. The name is derived from *platina* meaning little silver. Platinum is often found in granules or small nuggets in placer deposits. There are major deposits in the USSR, Canada, and S. Africa but most are of very low concentration.

ROUNDED
Platinum is quite soft (H=4–4.5) so it is unusual to find sharp crystals. These cubic crystals come from Sierra Leone.

CROWN OF PLATINUM
The crown of Queen Elizabeth the Queen Mother is made of platinum. It is part of the British Crown Jewels.

RICH LAYER
This piece of platinum-bearing pyroxenite comes from a layer of igneous rock in South Africa called the Merensky reef. This layer is only about 30 cm (12 in) thick but is very rich in platinum.

UNUSUALLY LARGE
Nuggets of platinum are not often as large as this one from the Ural Mountains, USSR. It weighs 1.1 kg (2.4 lb).

Silver

Crystals of silver are rare, but cubic crystals are occasionally found. Silver usually occurs massive or as thick wiry aggregates. In medieval times, silver was more valuable than gold. It was the main metal used for money and was also used for fine metal-work having a hardness of only 2.5–3. Today, metallic silver is used in electronics, silver plating, and jewellery, and a huge amount is used in the photographic industry (p. 63).

MEDIEVAL MINE
In medieval times the area around Sainte Marie, Alsace, France, was one of the richest silver-mining areas in Europe. This illustration from a medieval manuscript shows miners removing silver ore from one of the mines.

IN NEED OF A POLISH
This dendritic growth (p. 23) of silver crystals is slightly tarnished. It comes from the Huantajaya mines, in Chile.

SILVER WIRE
One of the most famous localities for silver was Kongsberg in Norway. These thick wire-like crystals of silver, with white crystals of quartz and calcite, are from there.

VALUABLE BONUS
Silver is now mostly extracted as a byproduct from the mining of copper and lead-zinc deposits such as galena, a lead sulphide. These fine crystals of galena come from Silvermines, Co. Tipperary, Eire.

Animal and vegetable

GEMS DERIVED FROM ANIMALS AND PLANTS are described as organic. They include amber, jet, coral, pearl, and shell. They are not as hard (4 or less) or as dense (1.04 – amber to 2.78 – pearl) as gemstones but have been popular for thousands of years because of their beauty. Beads of shell and amber have been found in ancient graves dating from 2000 B.C. Pearls have long been symbols of beauty and purity and greatly valued. The Roman emperor Julius Caesar is said to have paid the equivalent of about £150,000 ($350,000) for a single pearl.

PREHISTORIC GEMS
In the Jurassic period, 160 million years ago, dinosaurs and other giant reptiles lived among the trees which produced amber and jet.

Jet and amber

Jet and amber both come from trees. Jet is a fine-grained, black rock formed over millions of years from rotted and compressed trees, in a similar way to coal. Amber is the fossilized resin, or sap, of trees that lived as much as 300 million years ago.

JET LAGGED
This piece of jet shows its origin. It contains fossils of several long-extinct animals including an ammonite. Unlike coal it is hard-wearing and can be polished.

Fossil ammonite

ANCIENT TRAVELLER
The major source of amber is the south and east coast of the Baltic sea. Amber is only slightly denser than sea water and large lumps can be carried long distances across the sea. This specimen was found on the east coast of England.

Coral

Coral is a skeleton of calcium carbonate made by colonies of soft-bodied animals which live in tropical or sub-tropical waters. The range of colours, from black to blue to cream to red, is due to different growth conditions and organic contents.

Carving from Mediterranean coral of a monkey clinging to a branch

Coral living in a tropical sea

ANCIENT VALUES
These branches of the highly prized red coral are from the Mediterranean species *Corallium rubrum*. It was greatly valued by the Ancient Romans.

NECKLACE MATERIAL
This blue coral comes from the species *Heliopora caerules* which grows in the seas around the Philippines. It is often cut into beads for necklaces.

Pearl and shell

The sheen on pearls and the inside of some shells is caused by light reflecting on tiny platelets of calcium carbonate called nacre. Pearls, found in some marine and freshwater shells, form when a foreign body such as a sand grain becomes lodged inside the shell. To stop it irritating, the animal slowly surrounds it with nacre.

OYSTER CATCHERS
For more than 2,000 years the Persian Gulf has supplied the most beautiful natural pearls. The oysters (*Pinctada vulgaris*) used to be recovered by teams of divers. Today many pearls are cultured. An irritant is put into the oysters and the shells are farmed for their pearls.

PEARLS OF COLOUR
Pearls come in many colours including blackish, golden yellow, pink, cream, and white.

BUNCH OF PEARLS
Bombay has been a centre of pearl drilling for centuries. Some were sold as a "Bombay bunch". Each size was strung separately on silk, then combined with strings of other sizes suitable for a necklace, and finished off with tassels of silver wire.

MAXIMUM SIZE
The best pearls come from oysters and mussels. *Pinctada maxima* is the largest pearl oyster. It is found in the seas around Australia and Malaysia.

Mother of pearl

Iridescent nacre

CANNING JEWEL
Irregularly shaped pearls are called baroque pearls. There are four, including a magnificent one forming the body, in the Canning Triton jewel. It was probably made in south Germany in the late 16th century and is now in the Victoria and Albert Museum in London.

Baroque pearl

SHELL SHINE
Shells with brightly coloured blue and green nacre belong to the family *Haliotis*. They are found in American waters where they are called abalone, and in the seas around New Zealand where they are called paua.

Pill box with an abalone lid

What is it worth?

THE MARKET VALUE OF GEMS plays a large part in persuading people to buy them. Fashions change, so that gems that were priceless in the 19th century may no longer be so and vice-versa. Further back in time, lapis lazuli, turquoise, agates, and emerald were prized. From the fifth to the 14th century A.D. stones were not often cut because this was thought to destroy their magic. Since then however, more and more stones have been cut to enhance their beauty, and they are traded to satisfy people's desire to display their style or wealth. Since medieval times diamond, ruby, pearl, emerald, and sapphire have been popular, while the popularity of species such as topaz, garnet, and aquamarine has been erratic.

WHAT PRICE?
Gem values can vary widely, even within one species, according to colour, clarity, and cut. This 57.26-carat sapphire is of such extraordinary size and fine colour that it can only be valued if it changes hands.

TRAVELLING SALESMAN
Jean Baptiste Tavernier was a remarkable Frenchman who lived in the 17th century. He travelled in Europe and Asia, buying and selling gems. His accounts of his travels are in such detail that they are used to research the origins of famous diamonds.

Cut synthetic ruby

1-carat ruby

Carob seed

Carob pod

PRICELESS
Painite is priceless. Only three crystals are known, and none have yet been on the open market. It was found in Myanmar by the gem dealer A.C.D. Pain and when confirmed as a new species, was named after him.

Synthetic ruby crystals

NOT CHEAP
Time and care are needed to grow good synthetic crystals (pp. 26–27) and the equipment is expensive. Stones cut from such crystals are therefore not cheap, but natural stones of similar colour still cost 10 to 100 times more.

WEIGHT IN BEANS
The seeds of the carob tree are of remarkably constant weight, and they were used for many centuries as a standard for comparing the weights of precious stones. Later, a standard weight similar to that of the carob seed was used, and it was called the carat. For some time it was slightly different in different trading centres, but early this century a metric standard of 0.2 g (0.006 oz) was agreed internationally.

DOUBLED UP
A stone made of two materials glued or fused together is known as a doublet. Triplets have three layers – the central one being coloured glass or cement. The most popular doublet is the garnet-topped doublet (GTD). The top is a thin piece of colourless garnet which is more durable than the glass base which provides the colour. These cheaper stones are sometimes sold by disreputable traders as rubies, sapphires, or emeralds.

Chipped glass of a GTD

THEFT PREVENTION
This 1910 photograph shows Chinese sorters in the ruby mines of Mogok, Myanmar. The sorters were made to wear wire helmets to stop them stealing rubies by hiding them in their mouths while they were sorting.

SHORT-LASTING
Red glass has long been used to imitate ruby, but its lustre and shape soon deteriorate with age. In contrast, ruby with its greater hardness and toughness keeps these qualities for much longer.

Synthetic
rutile

Strontium
titanate

Fluorite

Quartz

STONE SUBSTITUTES
Diamond is the most frequently imitated stone in jewellery as there are many people who cannot afford the real thing. The oldest imitations are glass and rock crystal, but in the 20th century synthetic garnets and then cubic zirconia became available. This selection of diamond simulants is arranged clockwise in order of increasing fire, beginning with fluorite.

Lithium
niobate

Topaz

Cubic
zirconia

Synthetic
sapphire

GGG (gadolinium
gallium garnet)

Diamond

Synthetic
spinel

YAG (yttrium
aluminium
garnet)

Zircon

Glass

JUST LIKE THE REAL THING
This advertisement was for Faulkner's Celebrated Diamonds. They were advertised as "The only perfect substitute for diamonds of first water".

Measurements are given in millimetres and the details of proportions, clarity, and colour are listed

Clarity and colour are graded on a scale. This diamond is graded SI$_1$ (small inclusion) for clarity and G (near colourless) for colour

MILLION-DOLLAR MAN
The most valuable stones on the market in the past ten years have been diamonds, rubies, and emeralds, but even the most expensive diamond was only a fraction of the record price paid for Van Gogh's *Portrait of Dr Gachet*. This was sold at Christies, New York, in May 1990 for $82.5m (£49.1m).

FOUR Cs
Two diamonds that look alike at first can have very different values. Four characteristics that determine their value are known as the four Cs: cut, weight in carats, colour, and clarity. In the 1930s, the Gemological Institute of America established its own system of grading and issued certificates for individual diamonds containing information about the four Cs. Different systems were introduced in Europe but in 1975 the grading procedure started to be standardized.

The positions of any inclusions are indicated on the outlines of the crown and pavilion

Polystyrene
latex

Real black
opal

Gilson
opal

Slocum
stone

MADE TO MATCH
Opal is imitated in several ways. The flamboyant Slocum stone is made of glass and is much cheaper than true opal. Gilson opal is grown in the laboratory over many months and is intermediate in value. True opal is graded according to body colour and the play of colours, with black opal being the rarest and most expensive.

Making them sparkle

SOME ROUGH CRYSTALS are beautifully shaped and have breathtaking lustre and colour, but most are worn down or have other surface imperfections. A skilled stone cutter and polisher, called a lapidary, can turn these stones into objects of beauty and value by using their individual qualities in the right way. Beads and cabochons are the oldest cuts for such materials as lapis lazuli and turquoise (p. 50), and carnelian and agate (p. 33). Brilliant-cut diamonds are known from the 17th century and this is the most popular cut today.

BRILLIANT-CUT RUTILE
In 1919 Marcel Tolkowsky set down the precise angles and proportions of a brilliant cut to give the best combination of sparkle, brilliance, and fire.

ROSE-CUT SMOKY QUARTZ
The rose cut dates from the 14th century. Most stones have a flat base and a shallow or deep dome-shaped top covered in triangular facets.

TABLE-CUT AMETHYST
The table cut is derived from the diamond octahedron by sawing off the top above what becomes a square or rectangular girdle.

STEP-CUT QUARTZ
The step cut has many rectangular facets. It is particularly suitable for strongly coloured gems such as emerald and tourmaline.

Cutting a brilliant

A lapidary first studies a rough stone with a powerful lens called a loupe. This shows the direction of grain and the flaws. The stone is marked to show where it should be sawn and the facets are then ground.

Crown

Bezel

Girdle

Pavilion

Table facet

1 ROUGH CHOICE
A rough crystal is chosen for cutting.

2 SAWN IN TWO
The crystal is sawn to remove the top pyramid and rounded by grinding against another diamond, called bruting. (The cutting sequence is shown here with models.)

BRILLIANT TRANSFORMATION
The Koh-i-noor diamond (p. 35) was recut into a brilliant in 1852. Here the Duke of Wellington makes the first facet, watched by Mr Voorsanger, the cutter from Amsterdam.

The Koh-i-noor cut as a brilliant

3 FACETING BEGINS *left*
The stone is mounted on a stick called a dop and the first facet – the flat table – is ground on a cast-iron wheel, called a scaife, followed by more facets.

4 FURTHER FACETS *left*
Four bezel facets are ground between the table and the girdle. The stone is turned over and four facets ground on the pavilion. A further four facets are ground on the crown and on the pavilion, and the culet facet on the base.

AMSTERDAM STREET SCENE
BY PETRUS BERETTA (1805-1866)
In the 17th century, Amsterdam became the most important centre in the world for trading and cutting diamonds and retained a prominent position until the 1930s.

5 FINISHED OFF *right*
The stone is finished by the brillianteer who adds 24 facets above and 16 below the girdle. The standard brilliant has 57 facets or 58 with a culet.

Diamond cutter's table of the 1870s

Agate

Amethyst

Triangular-cut citrine

Irregular-cut sapphire

Heart-cut heliodor

CUTTING IT FINE
These craftsmen from Perth, Australia, are cutting diamonds from the Argyle mine (p. 25). Diamond-cutting tools remained virtually unchanged from the 15th century until the development of automatic machines in the 1970s, and later, lasers.

OLD FASHION
Beads can be made out of relatively soft materials and are among the oldest forms of fashioned gems. They are made today using automatic machines.

LIGHT DISPLAY
Star sapphires and rubies (p. 37) must be cut as cabochons if the tiny needles of rutile inside are to reflect the light and display the star.

SPECIAL CUTS
If a stone is very rare a special cut may be developed to keep as much weight as possible. Or stones may be given unusual cuts for special occasions.

HARD-HEADED
Hard-wearing opaque materials such as this garnet are often cut into rounds or ovals with plain, curved surfaces. These are called cabochons – a French word derived from the Latin _cabo_ meaning a head.

Cabochons of quartz, cut to display the eye effect and set in a brooch

Groove caused by polishing garnet cabochons

OVER AND OVER
Rocks and minerals can be polished by tumbling them in a drum with water and grit. The kind of grit depends on the material to be polished, and ranges from coarse grits to start with, to fine grits to finish off with.

INDIAN POLISH
This massive corundum was used in India in the 19th century for fashioning and polishing garnets. Continual use has caused tiny chips to split off, eventually leaving grooves.

GRINDING AWAY
The grinders in this 20th-century agate-grinding workshop are holding the stones against large water-driven grinding wheels, charged with abrasive powder.

Lore and legends

SUPERSTITION, MYTH, and romance, have been attached to crystals since ancient times. In Persian mythology the world is said to stand on a giant sapphire, the reflection of which colours the skies blue. Emeralds were once thought to blind snakes, and wondrous medicinal properties have been given to diamonds. Rubies were symbols of power and romance in the Middle Ages, and ladies often presented jewels to their knights as love tokens. Many specific stones are said to have been put under a terrible curse and stories are told of how some, such as the Hope Diamond, bring disaster to their owners.

CRYSTAL COMPASS
Some sources say that the Vikings navigated with transparent cordierite crystals. When held up to sunlight and rotated, cordierite darkens and changes colour. Using this property, the Vikings would have been able to work out compass directions.

BRAINY BIRDS
The mystery of how a bird migrates may have been solved. It is thought that a tiny magnetic crystal in its brain detects the earth's magnetic field.

POWER TO REPEL
Some pieces of magnetite, a naturally occurring iron oxide, are magnetic. They are known as lodestones and people in ancient times believed they had special powers. For example, it is said that Alexander the Great, a famous general of the third century B.C., gave lodestones to his soldiers to repel evil spirits.

Iron filings attracted to magnetite fan out to follow magnetic lines of force

Magnetite crystals

SOBERING INFLUENCE
Amethyst was supposed to have many useful powers in the 15th century, but its traditional virtue was its ability to cure drunkenness. One way in which it may have gained this reputation is that drinking vessels were sometimes made of amethyst. In these, water would look like red wine, but could be drunk with no intoxicating effect!

HOLY ROWS
The original breastplate of the High Priest of Israel is described in the Bible (Exodus 28, 15–30) as set with four rows of three stones. The stones are all named and include familiar species but some names are misleading. An example is the sapphire. This is described in detail elsewhere and is evidently what we now know as lapis lazuli.

STONE TEARS
Crystals of staurolite sometimes twin at right angles to form crosses. These used to be called *lapis crucifer* and were used as amulets at baptisms. In Patrick County, Virginia, USA, where fine examples have been found, these twin crystals are known as fairy stones. The legend is that they crystallized from the tears of fairies, who cried when they learned of the death of Christ.

Crystal gazing

Crystal balls have been used for telling the future since Greek and Roman times. The fortune teller looks at the polished surface of the ball intently until they can no longer focus on the ball but see instead a curtain of mist. This enables the gazer to see "visions" in the ball, imagined in response to questions asked by the person whose fortune is being told.

VISIONARY
John Dee was a charlatan of the 16th century but a favourite of Queen Elizabeth I of England. He conducted many crystal gazings in which a colleague, Kelley, interpreted "visions" in the crystal.

FOR THE FUTURE
Quartz is the most popular material for crystal balls but other materials which have a shiny surface, such as mirrors, polished steel, and even the surface of water, have been known to have a satisfactory effect.

EASTERN PROMISER
Crystal balls have been found from cultures in the Far East, the Americas, and Europe. This one comes from China.

Birthstones

The dedicating of a special stone to each month of the year was first suggested in the 1st century A.D., and was linked to the twelve stones in the High Priest's breastplate. The custom of wearing such stones became popular in the 18th century. It started in Poland and then spread throughout Europe and the rest of the world.

December – Turquoise

January – Garnet

February – Amethyst

November – Topaz

October – Opal

March – Aquamarine

September – Sapphire

April – Diamond

May – Emerald

Rock crystal engraved with the twelve signs of the zodiac

August – Peridot

July – Ruby

June – Pearl

ON THE CARDS
Signs of the zodiac have also been given their own gemstones. These cigarette cards of 1923 show carnelian representing Virgo and peridot representing Leo.

WILLS'S CIGARETTES

WILLS'S CIGARETTES

LEO

VIRGO – THE VIRGIN

CHANGING MONTHS
The gem species which represent each month have varied considerably throughout history. The Roman, Arabian, Jewish, and Russian cultures all favoured different combinations. The group shown here is the most popular today.

Crystals at home

MANY EVERYDAY OBJECTS in the home are crystalline. There are ice crystals in the freezer, salt and sugar crystals in the food cupboard and in food itself, crystals of vitamin C and aspirin in the medicine cupboard, tartrate crystals in the wine bottle, and silicon crystal chips in the fridge and washing machine. The TV, telephone, radio, and camera work because of crystals, the house is built of materials which are mostly crystalline, and outside, bikes and cars stand slowly rusting – crystallizing!

BY A WHISKER
"Hello. This is London. Here is the news." This might be what these ladies are listening to using a crystal set. In this early form of wireless, operators moved a thin copper wire, sometimes known as a cat's whisker, against a galena crystal to pick up radio waves. Crystal sets became popular in the 1920s when public broadcasting began.

FOR THE RECORD
In some record players, there are two crystals. The stylus is made of hard-wearing diamond or corundum, and a piezoelectric crystal (p. 31) in the cartridge converts vibrations received from the record into an electrical charge.

Diamond stylus

Enlarged photograph of a diamond stylus travelling through the groove on a stereo record

SPOONFUL OF SUGAR
Over 100 million tonnes of sugar are crystallized every year in refineries. Sugar is extracted as a liquid solution from raw sugar cane or beet, then converted into sugar crystals. The silver spoon holding these sugar crystals is itself a mass of silver crystals.

Liquid crystal display

Greatly enlarged photograph of crystals of vitamin C

CRYSTAL DISPLAY
The displays in many calculators are liquid crystal displays (LCD). Liquid crystals are not truly crystalline. They flow like a liquid but have molecules arranged like those of crystals and some properties of crystals. Power rearranges the molecules so that they reflect or absorb light and show dark or light.

VITAL INTAKE
These tablets contain crystals of ascorbic acid, or vitamin C. Ascorbic acid is a white crystalline substance present in plants, especially citrus fruits, tomatoes, and green vegetables. Vitamins are essential to us in small quantities. They cannot be produced by the body, and therefore have to be taken in through food or tablets.

PRECIOUS STONES
Many people own jewellery some of which may contain precious or semi-precious stones. This silver brooch contains diamonds, a blue sapphire, and a pearl.

Photo enlargement of needle-like crystals in kettle fur

KETTLE FUR
Crystals can be found in your kettle. Even after purification processes there are still some harmless minerals dissolved in tap water. These crystallize and coat the inside of your kettle when the water is boiled.

ON FILM
When a photograph is taken, an image is recorded on light-sensitive material by the action of light. Most film uses light-sensitive crystals of silver salts. The photographic industry is one of the largest users of silver.

PRESSED FOR TIME
Many watches use tiny quartz crystals to control time (p. 31), and ruby is used for watch bearings. The ruby crystals are usually synthetic (pp. 26–27).

Ruby crystals

Photo enlargement of silver nitrate crystals on a photographic film

Hand lens for studying the major features of crystals

Collecting
Crystal collecting can be enjoyed without spending too much money. Crystals can be collected in the field, bought, or exchanged with friends and dealers. They are usually fragile and should be carefully stored. Those found in the field should be curated with details of where they were found and, if possible, their host rock.

Wulfenite crystal

IN MINIATURE
A popular method of collecting and storing crystals is as micromount specimens a few millimetres in size. They take up little space and fine crystal groups of rare and unusual minerals can be collected.

Amethyst crystals

CAVITY FILLERS
Crystal-lined geodes are often found within basaltic lava flows. They are formed from fluids which percolate through the rocks and crystallize in available cavities. They may be highly prized by collectors.

FIELD WORK
Use a geological hammer to collect in the field. Wear suitable clothing and boots, a hard hat, and eye protector. Ask permission to collect on private land and always observe the country code.

Did you know?

AMAZING FACTS

In ancient times, the Persians thought the Earth rested on a giant sapphire and that the blue of the heavens was its reflection. Others thought the sky was a sapphire in which the Earth was set.

Sapphire and diamond pendant

Sapphire-blue is a colour associated with the qualities of harmony, trust and loyalty. This is the reason why women in many countries choose sapphires as the stones in their engagement rings.

The name 'garnet' comes from the Latin for pomegranate, a fruit which has bright red, garnet-like seeds. In fact, the colour of garnets varies from violet-red to the deepest wine.

Pomegranate

Diamonds are sometimes found under the sea. People trawl for diamonds off the coast of Namibia in southern Africa. The latest techniques involve large offshore ships pumping gravel containing diamonds up to the surface.

Since diamond was discovered in kimberlite rock, it has been extracted on a massive scale. Over 25 tonnes of rock have to be blasted for every finished carat - 0.2 g (0.007 oz) - of diamond mined.

In medieval times, people who could afford it wore a diamond jewel to protect them from the plague. The Ancient Greeks thought that diamonds could protect people from poisons.

Moonstones are often set in silver, to bring out their silvery sheen.

Moonstone necklace

People once thought that a moonstone's opalescent lustre waxed and waned just like the moon, so moonstones have always been worn by worshippers of the moon.

Topaz crystals can be up to a metre (3.28 ft) long and weigh several hundred kilos. The name 'topaz' is thought to come from the Sanskrit word *tapas*, which means 'fire'.

The Ancient Greeks thought that amber was the hardened rays of a sunset and it was considered sacred to the sun god Apollo. Amber can produce an electric charge when rubbed. In fact, the word 'electricity' comes from the Greek word for amber, *elektron*.

Diamond dredging boats

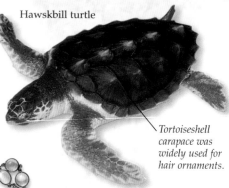

Hawskbill turtle

Tortoiseshell carapace was widely used for hair ornaments.

Tortoiseshell doesn't come from a tortoise at all, but from a turtle. It is made from the shell of the rare Hawksbill turtle, which is now a protected species. Most 'tortoiseshell' in jewellery nowadays is made of plastic.

Six-rayed star sapphires were once thought to provide the best protection from evil. The three crossing arms of the star were meant to represent faith, hope, and destiny.

Star sapphire

To the Egyptians, the intense blue of lapiz lazuli meant that it was a heavenly stone. They often used it on statues of their gods and in burial masks, to protect them in the next life.

The Arabians thought that pearls were the tears of gods. Although cultivating pearls (making them grow by putting irritants into oysters) is much faster than waiting for natural pearls to form, it can still take a very long time - up to 4 years.

QUESTIONS AND ANSWERS

Q How long have people been mining for gemstones?

A Jewellery has been found in burial sites dating back thousands of years. Ancient jewellery is rare, but some Ancient Egyptian pieces have survived. These are often made of gold set with gems such as turquoise, lapis lazuli and carnelian.

Q What are potato stones?

A Potato stone is a name given to a geode, a hollow ball of rock encrusted inside with amethyst or other crystals. The crystals form when silica-rich liquids seep into gas bubbles in volcanic lava and magma as they cool. Also known as thunder eggs, geodes are highly prized.

Potato stones

Q Why are gemstones so precious?

A Gemstones are valuable because of their natural beauty, their durability, their rarity, and the way in which they are cut and polished. There are 3,000 different kinds of mineral, but only about 100 could be classed as gemstones, making them very rare.

Q Where do diamonds come from?

A Diamond forms at extremely high temperatures and pressure 80 km (50 miles) or more below the ground in the Earth's mantle. When diamonds were first discovered, 2,000 years ago, they were mainly found in river gravel. These days, most diamond is mined from kimberlite rock. Australia is the main producer today, but diamonds are also mined in Africa, the former USSR, Brazil and the USA.

Q What are seed pearls?

A Pearls vary in size, the smallest of all being seed pearls. Pearls are not weighed in carats like other gemstones, but in grains. One grain = 0.05 g (0.002 oz). Seed pearls weigh less than 0.25 of a grain.

Scarab beetle good-luck charm, found in Tutankhamun's tomb

Q Why were children often given coral jewellery in the past?

A Coral was thought to protect the person wearing it from evil. For this reason, children were often given coral necklaces and bracelets to keep them healthy and safe from harm.

Q Why are emeralds green?

A The characteristic green colour of emeralds come from tiny amounts of cromium and vanadium.

The Archduke Joseph Diamond and necklace

Q Why are gemstones cut and polished?

A Cutting and polishing gemstones transforms them into jewels. It maximizes the amount of light they reflect so that they sparkle and shine.

Q Why are organic gems often carved rather than cut into facets?

A Organic gems, such as coral, ivory, amber, jet and pearl are softer than mineral gems and are often opaque. For this reason, they are often carved and polished. Light cannot shine through them, so it is pointless cutting them into facets to increase their brilliance.

Q What is the connection between rubies and emery boards?

A Rubies are one of the most expensive gems. Ruby is a variety of the mineral corundum, which is second in hardness to diamond. Emery is an impure form of corundum and has been used as an abrasive for thousands of years.

Cut ruby

Q Which famous ruby isn't really a ruby at all?

A Many crown jewels around the world contain massive red gemstones called spinels, that people mistook for rubies. The huge Black Prince's Ruby in the British Imperial State Crown is in fact a spinel, given to the Black Prince in 1367 by the King of Spain as a token of his appreciation.

Record Breakers

MOST VALUABLE GEMSTONE:
Diamonds are the most precious gem, famed for their fiery beauty, as well as for being the hardest mineral on earth.

BIGGEST DIAMOND:
The largest single rough diamond ever mined was the Cullinan diamond, found in 1905 in South Africa. It weighed 3,106 carats and was cut into 9 large and 96 smaller stones.

CUTTING MARATHON:
It took three polishers, working 14 hours a day, eight months to cut and polish the Cullinan 1 diamond. The stone is now set in the British Imperial Sceptre.

PRICELESS GEM:
Only three crystals of painite are known, and none of them has ever been sold, making them priceless.

BIGGEST BERYL CRYSTAL:
A beryl crystal found in Madagascar weighed 36 tonnes and was about 18 m (60 ft) long.

Identifying gemstones

To the untutored eye, many gemstones look alike. They are often similar in colour and are cut in much the same way. Here is a guide to the colour and characteristics of some of the most popular gemstones, both mineral and organic.

Emerald lizard

Mixed-cut citrine with the orange tinge often seen in this gem

CITRINE
Citrine is a yellow or golden form of quartz. Natural citrine (its name comes from the word "citrus") is pale yellow, but it is extremely rare.

Oval mixed-cut amethyst with a typical purplish violet colour

AMETHYST
Amethysts are purple, lilac or mauve quartz crystals. They often have distinctive internal markings and a blue or reddish tinge when seen from different angles.

A tiger's eye, cut and polished to show up its stripes

TIGER'S EYE
Tiger's eye is a variety of chalcedony, a type of quartz composed of tiny fibres. It has a waxy appearance and is black with yellow and golden-brown stripes.

Typical reddish orange polished stone from India

CARNELIAN
Also called cornelian, this is a translucent, reddish-orange or brown form of chalcedony.

Colourless, brilliant-cut diamond with black inclusions

DIAMOND
Made of pure carbon, diamond is exceptionally hard and shines brightly. It occurs in many colours, but the most popular variety is pure and colourless.

Cushion mixed-cut ruby in bright red

RUBY
One of the most expensive gems, the classic ruby is a rich red, but it can vary in colour from pink to brown. Rubies are second in hardness only to diamonds.

Pale blue Sri Lankan sapphire

SAPPHIRE
The most valuable sapphires are a clear shade of deep blue, but they can also be yellow, green, pink or colourless. Like ruby, sapphire is a type of corundum.

Bluish green emerald with many tiny fissures and internal markings

EMERALD
A variety of beryl, emeralds are a rich green. Only the finest gems are transparent and flawless. Most emeralds have flaws known as a *jardin*, the French for "garden".

Octagonal step-cut aquamarine with a slight greenish tinge

AQUAMARINE
Another variety of beryl, aquamarine ranges in colour from pale sea-green to dark blue. It can appear to change colour when viewed from different angles.

An opal displaying flashes of green and blue

OPAL
Opal is known for its iridescence and flashes of colour. Iridescent opal with a dark background is called black opal. "Potch opal" is opaque, without any iridescence.

Salmon-pink coloured topaz

TOPAZ
Topaz occurs in several different colours, ranging from deep golden yellow (known as sherry topaz) and pink to blue and green. Natural pink stones are extremely rare.

Watermelon tourmaline

TOURMALINE
Tourmalines come in a range of colours, but they all have the same crystal structure. Watermelon tourmaline is so called because of its pink and green colouring.

Pyrope (garnet) cut as an oval

GARNET

There are several different gemstones in the garnet group. The most popular for jewellery are the pyrope, which is blood-red, and the deep red almandine.

Octagonal mixed-cut peridot

PERIDOT

Peridot is an olive or bottle-green colour with a distinctive waxy lustre. It has strong double refraction, which means you can often see a doubling of the back facets.

A grey moonstone

MOONSTONE

The moonstone derives its name from its blue-white sheen, like moonshine. Some varieties are grey, yellow, pink or green.

Octagonal mixed-cut with a vitreous lustre

SPINEL

The most popular spinel is ruby-red, but it also occurs in blue and yellow. Until the 19th century, red spinels were known as Balas rubies, perhaps after their source.

Cut yellow chrysoberyl

CHRYSOBERYL

Chrysoberyl is renowned for its golden colour. One variety, called alexandrite, appears to change colour from green to light red when seen in artificial light.

Colourless zircon produced by heating a reddish-brown stone

ZIRCON

Pure zircon is colourless and resembles diamond, but it is more likely to be golden brown. Many zircons are heat-treated to produce blue or colourless gemstones.

Translucent jadeite with black inclusions

JADE

Two different minerals, jadeite and nephrite, are recognized as jade. The finest quality jadeite is emerald green. Nephrite varies in colour from cream to olive green.

Polished rock speckled with pyrite

LAPIS LAZULI

Prized for its intense dark blue, lapis lazuli is a rock made up of several minerals. Specks or streaks of pale pyrite and calcite are often visible against the blue.

Stone cut and polished as a cabochon

TURQUOISE

Turquoise is valued for its intense colour, which varies from blue–green to bright blue. Opaque, it is usually cut and polished into rounded beads or cabochons.

ORGANIC GEMSTONES

Unlike most other gemstones, which are mineral in origin, organic gems are derived from plants and animals. Amber, jet, coral, pearl, ivory and shell are all organics. These materials are not stones and they are not as hard and durable as mineral gems. Instead of being cut into facets like most other gemstones, they are usually polished or carved.

Carved jet with a finely wrought rose at the centre

JET

Jet is a fine-grained rock formed from fossilized wood. Black or very dark brown, it is opaque with a velvety lustre. Once popular for mourning jewellery, it is often faceted and polished to a high shine.

Transparent golden brown beads that have been faceted

Amber necklace

AMBER

Amber is formed from the hardened resin of trees. Transparent or translucent, it is usually a golden orange colour, but it can also be a rich dark red, and occasionally contains insects and plants.

Intricate red coral carving showing a monkey climbing a tree

CORAL

Coral is made of the remains of coral polyps. It can be pink, red, white or blue. Naturally dull, it shines when polished.

A roughly spherical pearl suitable to be used as a bead

PEARL

Pearls are formed in shellfish and have a characteristic iridescent sheen. They vary in colour from white and cream with a hint of pink to brown, or even black.

Find out more

The best way to find out more about crystals and gemstones is to visit museums. Natural history and geological museums usually have extensive rock and mineral displays and are an invaluable source of information on how crystals are formed and what they look like in their natural state. Many of them also have good gemstone collections. There are many different places where you can see how precious gems have been used in jewellery. Here are some suggestions for interesting places to visit, as well as a list of useful websites that will provide you with plenty more information.

CRYSTALS AND GEMSTONES
In most natural history and geological museums, such as the Earth Galleries at the Natural History Museum in London, there are wonderful displays of cut gemstones and famous jewels, specially lit to show them to their best effect. There are also excellent examples of crystals and gemstones in their natural state, often still embedded in their matrix (host) rock.

WHERE GEMSTONES ARE FOUND
Some mineral gemstones, such as quartz and garnet, are found all over the world. Others, such as diamonds, are far more rare. Where gemstones are found depends on particular geological conditions. This map shows the main locations around the world of 12 of the most popular and highly prized gems. If you visit any of these areas, you may be able to visit mines or see samples of the gemstones in local galleries, museums and shops.

KEY TO SYMBOLS

DIAMOND	RUBY	SAPPHIRE	EMERALD
AQUAMARINE	CHRYSOBERYL	TOPAZ	TOURMALINE
PERIDOT	GARNET	PEARL	OPAL

GEM COLLECTIONS
There are often private collections of gemstones on display in museums. You could start a gem collection of your own. Look for specimens on beaches, river banks and hillsides. Clean your finds with water and let them dry, then arrange them in empty matchboxes or small cardboard trays. Try taking them to your local museum for help in identifying them.

Cut gemstones that form part of the Mathews collection in London

USEFUL WEBSITES

- You can access the Earth lab database at the Natural History Museum for help identifying minerals at: **www.nhm.ac.uk/museum/earthlab**
- Rockwatch is an on-line club for young geologists: **www.rockwatch.org.uk**
- You can see great gems from the Smithsonian Gem and Mineral Collection at: **www.min.uni-bremen.de/sgmcol**
- The Geological Society's website is a good source of information: **www.geolsoc.org.uk**

Places to visit

THE EARTH GALLERIES AT THE
NATURAL HISTORY MUSEUM
Cromwell Road,
London SW7

THE VICTORIA AND ALBERT MUSEUM
(For jewellery)
Cromwell Road,
London SW7

GEM-ROCK MUSEUM,
Chain Road, Creetown,
Kirkcudbrightshire,
DG8 7HJ

THE NATIONAL MUSEUM OF NATURAL
HISTORY AT THE SMITHSONIAN
INSTITUTION
10th Street and Constitution Avenue, NW,
Washington DC 20560
USA

MUSÉE DU LOUVRE
Rue de Rivoli,
Paris 75001,
France

JEWELS AND JEWELLERY

A museum of decorative arts is a good place to see how gemstones have been set in jewellery over the ages. As well as historic pieces, modern jewellery in styles such as Art Deco are well worth looking at. To see examples of early jewellery, try visiting the Ancient Egyptian section of a museum. If you travel abroad, visit local craft museums to see samples of ethnic jewellery.

Napoleon 1 diamond necklace from the Smithsonian Institution, Washington

TOPKAPI PALACE TREASURY

If you go to Istanbul in Turkey, it is worth visiting the Topkapi Palace Museum, which has a magnificent collection of Colombian emeralds set in jewellery and other accessories. As well as the dagger below, the collection includes a golden throne studded with tourmaline, a carved emerald snuffbox and vases carved from exquisite green jadeite, a type of jade.

Dagger with emeralds set into the hilt

CROWN JEWELS

Impressive examples of famous gemstones set in gold and silver are on display in the Crown Jewels of France, Britain and Austria. At the Louvre in Paris, you can see the coronation crowns of Napoleon and Louis XV, as well as other magnificent crowns, sceptres and swords, some dating back as far as the Middle Ages. Also on view is the Regent, one of the purest diamonds in the world, which was worn by Louis XV at his coronation in 1722. The British Crown Jewels are on display at the Tower of London and include many jewels that are still used in state ceremonies today, such as St Edward's Crown, the crown of England, which is only used for coronations, and the Imperial State Crown, which contains the famous Black Prince's Ruby.

The figure at the top is of Charlemagne (742–814), king of the Franks.

Gold set with precious jewels

Crown of Empress Eugénie on display at the Louvre

Golden sceptre set with gemstones, made for Charles V in 1380

The Tower of London Education Centre in London, where school children can try on replicas of the crown jewels and royal cloaks, as well as armour.

Glossary

ALLOCHROMATIC A term meaning "other-coloured". It describes gems that are naturally colourless but are coloured by tiny amounts of impurities.

ALLUVIAL DEPOSITS Pieces of rock and mineral that have been separated from their host rock by weathering and have been deposited elsewhere by rivers and streams.

AMORPHOUS Without a regular internal atomic structure or external shape.

ASTERISM The star effect seen in some gemstones, such as rubies and sapphires, when they are cut into cabochons.

BIREFRINGENCE (DR) Double refraction, a property of some crystals in which light passing through them is split into two rays.

Brilliant cut diamond

BRILLIANT CUT The most popular cut for diamonds and many other stones. The standard brilliant has 57 facets, or 58 if the gem is cut with a flat face at the base.

CABOCHON A type of cut in which a gemstone is cut into a round or oval with a plain, domed upper surface.

Star ruby cut into a cabochon

CARAT The standard measure of weight for gemstones. One metric carat equals 0.2 g.

CHATOYANCY The tiger's eye effect shown by some stones, such as chalcedony, when they are cut into cabochons.

CLEAVAGE The way in which a crystal splits apart along certain well-defined planes according to its internal structure.

COMPOSITION The fixed or well-defined chemical make-up of a mineral.

COMPOUND A chemical compound is made of two or more elements joined together chemically, which can only be separated by heat or great pressure.

CORE The area of iron and nickel at the centre of the Earth.

CRUST The thin outermost layer of the Earth.

CRYSTAL A naturally occurring solid with a regular internal structure and smooth external faces.

CRYSTALLINE Having a crystal structure.

CUT The way in which a gemstone is cut into a number of flat faces called facets, or rounded and polished.

Calcite crystal

DENDRITES Fern-like growths of crystals found lining the cracks and joints in rocks.

DICHROIC A term used to describe a gem that appears to be two different colours when viewed from different directions.

DIFFRACTION The splitting of white light into its constituent colours.

Dendrites of the mineral pyrolusite

DOUBLET A composite stone made of two pieces cemented or glued together.

DURABILITY The capacity to last for a long time without wearing out.

EROSION The wearing away of the surface of the land and rocks by a moving medium, such as water, ice or the sea.

FACET One flat surface of a cut gemstone.

FACETING Cutting and polishing gems into flat surfaces called facets.

FIRE A term used for dispersed light. A gem with strong fire is unusually bright.

FLUORESCENCE Coloured light that radiates from a mineral when it is exposed to invisible ultra-violet light.

Fluorescent crystal

GEMSTONE A decorative mineral or organic substance prized for its beauty, durability and rarity.

GEODE A cavity within a rock that is lined with crystals that grow towards the centre.

GIRDLE The widest part around the middle of a cut stone, where the top half (the crown) and the bottom half (the pavilion) meet.

HABIT The shape in which a crystal naturally occurs. Crystal habit is a key factor in identifying minerals.

IDIOCHROMATIC A term used to describe minerals, such as sulphur, whose colour is part of their chemical composition

INCLUSIONS Markings or particles found within a mineral.

INTERGROWN When two or more minerals grow together and interlock.

Idiochromatic sulphur

IRIDESCENCE A rainbow-like play of colours on the surface of a mineral, similar to a film of oil on water.

LAPIDARY A professional craftsman who is skilled at cutting gemstones to obtain the best optical effect.

LAVA Magma from within the Earth that erupts to the surface from volcanoes.

Iridescent hematite crystals

LODESTONE A piece of magnetite, a naturally occurring magnetic iron-oxide.

LUSTRE The way in which a mineral shines. Its lustre is affected by the way in which light reflects off the surface of the mineral.

MAGMA Molten rock deep within the Earth, below its surface.

MANTLE The layer of the Earth between its core and its crust.

MASSIVE A term used to describe minerals that have no particular shape.

MATRIX A term for the main body of a rock.

METAMORPHOSE To undergo a complete change of structure and composition. In rocks, this is usually caused by the effects of heat or pressure, or a combination of both. No melting takes place.

MICROCRYSTALLINE A mineral structure in which the crystals are too small to be seen with the naked eye.

MINERAL A naturally occurring inorganic solid with regular characteristics, such as crystal structure and chemical composition.

MIXED CUT A gemstone cut in which the facets above and below the girdle follow different styles, usually a brilliant cut above and a step cut below.

MOHS' SCALE A scale devised by the Austrian mineralogist Friedrich Mohs that measures the hardness of minerals according to what they are able to scratch, on a scale from 1 to 10.

NACRE Tiny platelets of calcium carbonate that create the soft sheen on pearls and inside some sea shells as they reflect light.

OPALESCENCE Milky blue form of iridescence.

OPAQUE Does not let light pass through it.

ORGANIC GEM A gem made by, or derived from, one or more living organisms.

PEGMATITE Igneous rock that forms as the liquids from magma cool and that is made up of unusually large crystals.

PENDELOQUE CUT Lozenge-shaped cut often used for flawed gems.

PHANTOMS Regular inclusions that occur within a crystal, such as parallel growth layers.

PIZOELECTRICITY A property of quartz crystals. Pressure on a crystal creates positive and negative charges across the crystal.

PLEOCHROIC A term used to describe a gemstone that looks as if it is two or more different colours when viewed from different directions.

PRISMATIC A term used to describe a crystal that has a uniform cross-section. It is usually column-shaped and has six sides.

PROPERTY A characteristic of a mineral, crystal or gemstone, such as its colour or habit.

REFRACTIVE INDEX (RI) A measure of how light rays slow down and bend as they enter a gemstone. One of the properties used to identify gems.

RESIN A sticky substance from certain plants.

RHOMB A shape rather like a lopsided cube.

RIVER GRAVELS Deposits of minerals that have been broken away from their host rock and washed downstream.

ROCK A combination of mineral particles. Some rocks contain a variety of minerals and some only one. Rocks may be inorganic, chemical or biological in origin.

ROUGH A term for the natural state of a rock or crystal before it is cut or polished.

SCHILLER Sheen or iridescence.

SPECFIC GRAVITY (SG) A property of minerals that is defined by comparing the weight of a mineral with the weight of an equal volume of water.

SPECTROSCOPE An instrument used to identify different gemstones. It reveals the bands of light that a gemstone absorbs.

Magma

Coral, an organic gem

Rhomb

Nacre inside shell

STEP CUT A rectangular or square-shaped gemstone cut with several facets parallel to the edges of the stone. It is generally used for coloured stones.

STRIATION Parallel lines, grooves or scratches in a mineral.

SYMMETRY, AXIS OF An imaginary straight line through a crystal. If the crystal were rotated about this line, the same pattern of faces would occur a number of times in a full turn.

SYNTHETIC GEMSTONE An artificial stone made in a laboratory that has a chemical composition and properties similar to the natural gemstone from which it is copied.

Step-cut ruby

TABLE CUT A type of step cut with a square table facet and girdle and parallel square facets.

TRANSLUCENT Material that allows some light to pass through it.

TRANSPARENT Material that allows light to pass right through it; able to be seen through.

TWINNED CRYSTALS Two crystals of the same mineral that are joined together at a common plane, known as the twin plane.

VEIN An infilled joint, fissure or fault. Veins are often made of minerals.

VITREOUS A term used for the glass-like quality of some gemstones. It is used to describe a gem's lustre.

Twinned calcite crystals

Index

Acknowledgements

Dorling Kindersley would like to thank: Peter Tandy at the Natural History Museum for his expert advice and help; Karl Shone for additional photography (pp. 28-29, 62-63); De Beers Industrial Diamond Division for the loan of diamond tools (p. 29); Gemmological Association of Great Britain for the gem certificate (p. 57); Keith Hammond for the loan of the beryl crystal (p. 21); Nancy Armstrong for the loan of the prospector's brooch (p. 41); Jane Parker for the index.
Illustrations by Thomas Keenes.

The publisher would like to thank the following for their kind permission to reproduce their images:
Picture credits c=centre; b=bottom; l=left; r=right; t=top
Peter Amacher: 48cl; Ancient Art and Architecture Collection: 9cl; Archives Pierre et Marie Curie: 31bc; Art Directors & TRIP: 69cr; Aspect Picture Library/Geoff Tompkinson: 28br; Dr Peter Bancroft: 45cr; Bergakademie Freiberg: 12cl, 19br; Bibliotheca Ambrosiana, Milan: 13cr; Bibliotheque St. Die: 53cl; Bridgeman Art Library, London / New York: Egyptian National Museum, Cairo, Egypt 65c; 18tl, 52tr, 58bl; Bibliotheque Nationale, Paris: 42tr; Paul Brierley: 16cr; F. Brisse, "La Symetrie Bidimensionnelle et le Canada", Smithsonian Institution, Washington DC: 37tr, 39t, 42br, 69tr; Canadian Mineralogist, 19, 217-224 (1981): 13tc; British Geological Survey: 63br; A. Bucher/Fondation M.S.A.:30tl; Gordon Bussey: 62tl, /Bibl. Magazin, Paris: 60br; © Christie's Images Ltd: 27br, 64tl, 65cb; Christie's, New York: 57cl; Bruce Coleman/Michael Freeman 52c; Lawrence H. Conklin: 49bl; Corbis: 64b, 69br; Crown copyright: 46cr, 53tl, 58cr; De Beers: 29bl, 29tc, 34cr, 35br; Dorling Kindersley/Eric Crichton: 47tc, DK Picture Library: Natural History Museum 66c; e.t. archive: 41br; Mary Evans Picture Library: 7tr, 15tl, 23br, 24cl, 38/39c, 38bl, 46tr, 57tr, 58c, 61tr, 61bl; Fondation M.S.A.: 11tl; Michael Freeman: 25tc, 37c; Grukker & Zn, Netherlands: 28tr; Robert Harding Picture Library: 44tr, 51tl; Harvaard Mineralogical Museum: 20cl; Harvey Caphin Alaemeda, New Mexico: 50tr; Ernst A. Heiniger: 39br; Michael Holford: 7cl, 37br, 44cr, 50br; Image Bank/Lynn M. Stone: 33cr, /Lionel ASY-Schwart: 54bl; India Office: 36tr, 56tr; Kobal Collection: 35cr; Kodak Ltd: 63c; Kunsthistoriches Museum, Vienna. Photo: Courthault Institute of Art: 40tr; Lauros-Giraudon: 34bl; Mansell Collection: 15bl, 35cl, 45c, 54tr; Moebius/Exhibition Bijoux Cailloux Fous, Strasbourg: 10bc; Museum national, d'Histoire Naturelle, Paris: 48cr; Museum of Manking: 52bl; National Gallery 50bl; Natural History Museum: 15tr, 19tr, 19c, 33br, 40bc, 51br, 68tl /Frank Greenaway FRPS:11 bl, 21bc, /P.Krishna, SS Jiang and A.R. Land: 21tc, /Harry Taylor ABIPP 31br; National Portrait Gallery, London: 16c, 43tr; Northern Island Tourist Board: 22bl; Perham's of West Paris, Maine: 23tr; Phototake, NYC/Yoav Levy: 30cr; Katrina Raphaell: 31cr; Réunion Des Musées Nationaux Agence Photographique: Musee de Louvre 69bc, 69bl; Ann Ronan Picture Library: 27tc, 27cr, 55c; Royal Geographical Society: 36bl, 39tc, 56bl; S. Australian Dept of Mines and Energy/B.Sowry: 41tc; Science Photo Library: 9tr, 14bl, /Dr Jeremy Burgess: 6tr, 62c, 63tr, /ESA/PLI:8tl, /John Howard: 43cr, /Peter Menzel: 25c, /NASA: 26c, /David Parker: 9br, /Soames Summerhays: 8bl; Brian Stevenson & Co: 25bl, 59tc; Stockphotos: 20br; R. Symes: 20tr; Uffizi, Florence. Photo: Giraudon: 32cl; Victoria and Albert Museum: 51cr, 55bl; Werner Forman Archive: 61cl; Peter Woloszynski: 49cr; Zefa/Leidmann:32tr, /Luneski: 60cl.

Jacket Credits
Getty Images: C Squared Studios front main image.
All other images © Dorling Kindersley. For further information see: www.dkimages.com